W9-BWF-786

13.50

CHRIST IN ALL THINGS

CHRIST IN ALL THINGS

Exploring Spirituality
with Teilhard de Chardin

Ursula King

The 1996 Bampton Lectures

ORBIS BOOKS

Maryknoll, New York 10545

The Catholic Foreign Mission Society of America (Maryknoll) recruits and trains people for overseas missionary service. Through Orbis Books, Maryknoll aims to foster the international dialogue that is essential to mission. The books published, however, reflect the opinions of their authors and are not meant to represent the official position of the society.

Copyright © 1997 by Ursula King

Published by Orbis Books, Maryknoll, NY 10545-0308

All rights reserved. No part of this publication may be reproduced or transmitted in any form or by any means, electronic or mechanical, including photocopying, recording, or any information storage or retrieval system, without prior permission in writing from the publishers.

Queries regarding rights and permissions should be addressed to: Orbis Books, P.O. Box 308, Maryknoll, NY 10545-0308.

Manufactured in the United States of America

Library of Congress Cataloging-in-Publication Data

King, Ursula.
    Christ in all things : exploring spirituality with Teilhard de Chardin / Ursula King.
       p. cm.
    "The 1996 Bampton lectures."
    ISBN 1-57075-115-3 (alk. paper)
    1. Teilhard de Chardin, Pierre—Contributions in spirituality.
2. Spirituality—Catholic Church—History—20th century.
3. Mysticism—History—20th century. 4. Catholic Church—
Doctrines—History—20th century. I. Title.
BX4705.T39K55   1997
248'.092—dc21   96-52867
                                        CIP

Everyone is prepared to admit the importance of Christianity *in the past;* but what about the present? and still more of the future?
—"The Christian Phenomenon" (1950)

What we are all more or less lacking at this moment is a new definition of holiness.
—"The Phenomenon of Spirituality" (1937)

Contents

Preface

Many books deal with Christian spirituality but few refer to the French Jesuit scientist and mystic Pierre Teilhard de Chardin. Unfortunately it is little known how much he was concerned with spiritual matters and how passionately he was committed to the renewal of Christian spirituality in the modern world. Much of this is due to the widespread ignorance of his work and the relative difficulty in gaining access to his numerous writings, especially to his early essays written in the trenches of the First World War. These are perhaps least known of all, but they deserve to be much more widely read for it is in these early, very lyrical writings with their prayerful meditations that we discover the emergence of a powerful spiritual vision and gain insight into a spiritual practice of great depth and energy. It is a spirituality which embraces the earth and all living forms and is alight with the fire of the Spirit. There are few who write so concretely, with so much realism and evocative appeal to the senses, so much emphasis on world, body, and matter. A spirituality which is so holistic, so strong and nourishing for body, mind and spirit, deserves far more recognition and appreciation than it has been given so far.

I would like to invite the readers of this book to explore something of the power of this spirituality by learning about Teilhard's experience and reflections, about his encounter with God in our confusingly complex world, about his wrestling with questions and doubts, about the strength and courage of his faith, and about his dazzling discovery of the Divine, which he saw as the intimately loving presence of Christ in all things.

The following chapters are a revised version of the eight Bampton Lectures which I gave between January and May

1996 in the University Church of St. Mary in Oxford. I would like to thank the electors for the opportunity to give these lectures and express my gratitude for the generous hospitality and kindness offered to me by my different hosts during my regular, very enjoyable visits to the University of Oxford. Special thanks are due to the Vice-Chancellor, Dr. Peter North and his staff, for all the excellent arrangements made on my behalf.

The Bampton Lectures are a hallowed tradition going back to 1780, after having been founded by a bequest of the Reverend John Bampton. The list of lecturers is a long and distinguished one, and the series set such an example that in 1948 an American bequest was made for the additional establishment of Bampton Lectures at Columbia University, New York. This more recent bequest stipulates that "the subjects of the lectures at Columbia be concerned with theology, science, art or hygiene, and that at least every four years the lectures be theological."

The Bampton Lectures in Oxford are always entirely theological since the original will of the Reverend Bampton states clearly that "Eight Divinity Lecture Sermons" be preached upon a number of different subjects of which the first is "to confirm and establish the Christian Faith." I took this as my brief, for my research and teaching on Pierre Teilhard de Chardin have long convinced me that his life and thought are a powerful source for contemporary Christian renewal and a reaffirmation of the Christian faith in a world of science and technology.

Although revised, the chapters retain some of the style of the spoken lectures. They contain numerous quotations from Teilhard's essays in order to show how his ideas frequently anticipated so many of our own concerns. Even after eighty years—his first essay was written in 1916—his words retain a startling freshness and surprising newness which can make our spirit soar and provide many a seed for spiritual renewal and growth. The Lectures were intended to explore some of the ideas of an unusually complex and original thinker so that they may become better known and more widely debated, but they can in no way claim to be an exhaustive study of all Teilhard's creative thought on Christian spirituality. For this, far more time and space would be needed. This book presents only a modest selection from a rich *oeuvre* which amply repays any effort in studying it, and whose great inspirational powers remain to be discovered for further exploration and critical debate.

Passages from Teilhard's works are quoted from their published English translations which retain exclusive language throughout. Only occasionally have I chosen to give a different translation based on the original French text.

CHAPTER ONE

Christian Spirituality Today

Seeking Wholeness and Holiness

ᏮᎷᏍᎧ

Spirituality is of the greatest interest today. However differently understood in practice, spirituality is now widely discussed in both secular and religious contexts. We are experiencing a great revival in the attention paid to the spiritual classics of all faiths. But spirituality is not simply a phenomenon of the past; it is recognized as an important agent for personal and social transformation in the present. It also plays a significant part in interfaith dialogue, education, peace negotiations, the women's movement, ecology and other contemporary developments.

The current spiritual revival and interest in exploring the spiritual resources of different religious traditions occur in a global, cross-cultural and interfaith context. This deserves a study in itself, but in this book I am particularly concerned with the relevance and renewal of Christian spirituality in today's world. I will explore this theme by drawing on the ideas of the French scientist, Jesuit priest and mystic Pierre Teilhard de Chardin. This man may be considered without exaggeration one of the great Christians of the twentieth century, but his name is rarely mentioned by current writers on Christian spirituality. Yet his life and thought provide an admirable example of the strength and power that Christian faith can inspire in an age of science, critical doubt, and immense moral and ethical challenges.

Like other Christians of earlier ages, Teilhard recognized

1

the pressing need to relate Christianity to the culture and spirit of his own time. Today, with the existence of modern science, technology and an increasingly global world, this need is more pressing than ever. Early in his writing, at the end of the First World War, Teilhard wrote a brief essay pointing to the need for the "evangelisation of a new age."[1] He prefaced this essay with this statement: "The great converters, or perverters, of human beings have always been those in whom the soul of their age burnt *most intensely*."[2] Years later he spoke of the importance of finding a new understanding of the meaning of holiness, a new way of embodying the ideal of Christian perfection. In "Research, Work and Worship," written shortly before his death on April 10, 1955, he once again, for the last time in almost forty years of writing, emphasized the urgent need to combine "the fire of a new faith" in the world with the vision, the practice, the power of a religious faith. "We need a new theology," he wrote, "and a new approach to perfection, which must be gradually worked out in our houses of study and retreat houses, in order to meet the new needs and aspirations . . . But what we need perhaps even more . . . is for a new and higher form of worship to be gradually disclosed by Christian thought and prayer, adapted to the needs of tomorrow's believers without exception."[3]

He was passionately concerned with finding a homogeneity and coherence between science, religion and mysticism, a coherence for him best represented by Christianity and consisting in a deeply personal faith centered on the mystery of the Christian incarnation, through which all things cohere and find their center in Christ. But far from repeating Christian doctrines in a merely traditional manner, Teilhard felt immensely challenged by the advance of human thought and invention. He critically reflected on them and recognized their importance for our intellectual, moral and religious life. As he wrote in 1947 to the French philosopher Emmanuel Mounier: "When we speak of a 'theology of modern science,' it obviously does not mean that by itself science can determine an image of God and a religion. But what it does mean, if I am not mistaken, is that, given a certain development of science, certain representations of God and certain forms of worship are ruled out as *not being homogeneous* with the dimensions of the universe known to our experience. This notion of homogeneity is without doubt of central importance in intellectual, moral and mystical life."[4]

Teilhard wrestled with these questions and tried to find some answers, but he was not without doubt. However powerful and controversial his seminally fertile ideas are, however much criticized by scientists and theologians, his greatest and most lasting contribution lies no doubt in the strength and attraction of his spirituality and the inspiring way in which he lived the Christian faith. Spirituality held a central place in his thought, and because of the great significance of this subject, and the considerable role it plays in contemporary discussions, this book will explore different aspects of Christian spirituality, guided by the inspiration and concerns found in Teilhard's thought.

I begin by considering three questions: Why is spirituality important? What is meant by spirituality? Why is Teilhard de Chardin's thought of great significance for Christian spirituality today?

Why Is Spirituality Important?

Spirituality has become quite a fashionable word, although it is often unclear what people mean by it. It is used in both religious and secular contexts; in debates about religious education in schools; among theologians outside the Western world; among feminists, ecologists and peace workers; in politics and public debates; among people of different faiths and none.

The term "spirituality" is not new, as some seem to think, but has a long history in Christian life and theology. Modern Christian spirituality enjoys a continuity with the past, but it has also undergone some fundamental changes since the coming of modernity. It has been said that "the spiritual life has a history of its own which admits of epochal distinctions" and that there are some specific "religious characteristics which distinguish spiritual life in the modern age from that of an earlier period."[5]

Of all historical cultures, that of modernity is perhaps the most one-dimensional and the least open to transcendence.

Compared with the Christian Middle Ages, modernity initially brought a loss. Spiritual life, previously so central to a whole culture and so taken for granted, moved increasingly to a marginal position within society as a whole. Thus modern spirituality grew into a highly private mode of religious expression. We have seen the proliferation of all kinds of personal, mystical spirituality which have developed relatively independently, without an impact on the whole of society. The public domain of politics and economics is marked by the *absence* of spirituality, rather than its *presence*. But in strong contrast to this absence there are also many signs of a hunger and thirst for "things of the spirit," often expressed in very different and contrary ways.

Today our approach to human beings is primarily pragmatic. However, such an approach denies the need for self-transcendence, for a deeper, more reflective and contemplative awareness, for the discovery and exploration of a spiritual dimension that a Christian humanism sees as integral to all human beings. To what extent is our cultural ethos and education able to make us grow into true human beings? To what extent are we *under-humanized* or *de-humanized* in modern society rather than encouraged to develop our human potential to the fullest? This is one of the questions Teilhard was passionately interested in.

In an earlier age when Christian religious ideals still informed the entire culture, the human being was primarily understood in relation to the Divine, to God. The dominant scientific approach of today tends to relate the human being primarily to the animal and life worlds of the biosphere. Both approaches—that to the world of our natural environment and that to God—need to be combined and linked with each other in a way that is new and culturally transformative and creative. How can we develop a wholesome, truly world-affirming and culture-transforming spirituality? Perhaps it is the very questions and problems raised by modernity, and the possibilities opening up with new, postmodern perspectives, that will provide us with the opportunities for developing a truly holistic and transformative spirituality.

Contemporary spirituality is at a crossroads. It is not Christianity alone whose spirituality is being questioned. The knowledge and presence of Eastern religions in the West, the rise of new religious movements, the development of atheistic and agnostic humanisms, have all contributed to the questioning of traditional spiritualities. To achieve a new religious breakthrough, a genuine transformation of both consciousness and society, it is no longer enough to return to the past and revive ancient spiritual ideals and instructions. The increasing process of globalization affects the interchange of spiritual ideals as much as anything else and makes us conscious that humanity possesses a religious and spiritual heritage whose riches are indispensable for the creation of a much needed global religious consciousness.

Will the rise of such a consciousness lead to a new flowering of spirituality in an age of postmodernity? This is a question difficult to answer. One can only speculate about it, but I would like to argue that it will. There are numerous signs of a growing interest in spirituality, not only at the level of practice, in the growth of retreat houses, the increasing number of spiritual counselors and spiritual writings, but also at the theoretical level of critical debate and new understanding. Spirituality has now become an academic discipline, especially in the United States where a growing number of university courses on spirituality have come into existence over the last ten years or so, paralleled by the development of the academic Society for the Study of Christian Spirituality.[6] But spirituality can be studied in Britain too. There exists an M.A. in Christian spirituality at Heythrop College in the University of London while the University of Wales at Lampeter has introduced a new M.A. in Comparative Spirituality. This is concerned with studying the spiritual traditions of China, India, the Middle East and the Christian West. The Jesuit journal *The Way Supplement* has devoted its 1995 number to the topic "Teaching Spirituality,"[7] which raises the question of whether spirituality can not only be studied, but also be taught.

The most impressive scholarly achievement is probably the twenty-five-volume cross-cultural series World Spirituality, where each volume concentrates on a particular faith.[8] Its general editor, Ewert Cousins, stated in the preface to the series that this publication is forging a new discipline in the field of religion, namely the discipline of spirituality, which has its own central focus, categories and concepts, and its own distinct methodology. He writes:

> The transmission of spiritual wisdom may be the oldest discipline in human history. Yet this ancient discipline needs to be accorded its own place in academic studies; at the same time it must integrate the findings of other disciplines such as psychology, sociology, and critical historical research. The challenge of this series, then, has been to develop the academic methods, skills, and tools appropriate for this corpus of wisdom.
>
> The series has faced a second challenge: to deal with this discipline in a global context. We might say that there is emerging a new discipline: global spirituality. Such a discipline would study spirituality not merely in one tradition or one era but in a comprehensive geographic and historical context. And it would take into account this vast body of data not in isolation but in interrelationship. In this sense, the present series is attempting not merely to retrieve an ancient discipline in a modern academic mode but to lift it into a global context.[9]

This quotation highlights the importance of spirituality as a topic of study and research in contemporary academic circles. In Oxford it is especially the Alister Hardy Research Center, now at Westminster College, that has made considerable efforts over the years to study spiritual experience in modern society. But debates about spirituality in Britain have been stimulated more than anything else by the requirements of the 1988 Education Reform Act, which stipulates clearly that state schools must foster not only the intellectual, but also the spiritual and moral development of children across the entire school curriculum. This is an issue of great importance, not only for Britain but for other systems of education too, whether in North America, South Africa or elsewhere.

But how is this to be done? And what criteria should be applied? Much current work among teachers and their mentors is devoted to these questions. Perhaps leading in the field is the Christian Education Movement's Templeton Project, a two-year initiative launched in 1995 to foster spiritual development in a secular educational context in the classroom. Appropriate curriculum materials have been developed and the implications for the training of teachers will be considered.[10] This example shows how important it is to reflect on the nature and significance of spirituality.

But how are we to understand spirituality in the first place?

What Is Meant by "Spirituality"?

The subject matter of spirituality can be considered a perennial human concern, but from what I have said it is clear that the critical, comparative reflection on spirituality in a global context is a very recent phenomenon. The search for a clearer definition of this notoriously vague and general word "spirituality" is also of recent origin. In a traditional Christian context, spirituality was closely connected with the celebration of the Christian mysteries, particularly the eucharist, and it is linked with Christian ideals of holiness and perfection, preached by the gospel. The word spirituality eventually found its way into different European languages and, according to the Oxford English Dictionary, from 1500 onward spirituality could mean "the quality or condition of being spiritual; attachment to or regard for things of the spirit as opposed to material or worldly interests."[11] Here we have already the indication of a strong polarity, often developed into a sharp and mutually exclusive dualism, whereby the spiritual is seen as distinct from, and frequently opposed to, the material, bodily, and temporal. In Christianity, but also in other religions, the spiritual ideal is often embodied in groups of ascetics, monastics and renouncers with a strong tradition of denying the value of the body and of the world.

Many religions possess no precise word for spirituality. By way of example, I mention an experience in Taiwan where I was told in early 1996, when lecturing on contemporary women's spirituality, that the word "spirituality" does not exist in Chinese, but that people in Taiwan were nevertheless much involved in discussing "spiritual values" with regard to forthcoming political elections in the country. The different presidential candidates were apparently all seeking the blessings of spiritual leaders, particularly that of an important Buddhist nun whose influence over people seemed stronger than that of the politicians.

This is a good example of the interaction between the spiritual and the political. Beyond its Western, Christian origin, the concept of spirituality has now become universalized and is used as a code word to indicate a search for direction, meaning and spiritual values. The spiritual is often understood as an inward quest in contrast to the material, physical and external. This is certainly so in many traditional contexts of spirituality.

Some understand the spiritual as wider, more diffuse and less institutionalized than the religious; others consider the spiritual the very center and heart of religion, particularly expressed through religious and mystical experience. In order to get away from a dualistic and falsely idealized understanding of spirituality, quite a few authors make an effort to provide a more integral and inclusive definition. In recent works spirituality has been described as an attempt to grow in sensitivity—to self, to others, to nonhuman creation and to God—or as an exploration into what is involved in becoming human. In this sense spirituality is related to the quest for full humanity. Sandra Schneiders has described spirituality as "that dimension of the human subject in virtue of which the person is capable of self-transcending integration in relation to the Ultimate, whatever this Ultimate is for the person in question. In this sense, every human being has a capacity for spirituality or is a spiritual being."[12]

Here the term spirituality is applied to a dimension of all human beings, to the actualization of that capacity, and also to the study of that dimension. It is also in this sense that the Templeton Project uses a broad, inclusive interpretation of spiritual development taken from a British educational publication:

Spiritual development relates to that aspect of inner life through which pupils acquire insights into their personal existence which are of enduring worth. It is characterised by reflection, the attribution of meaning to experience, valuing a non-material dimension to life and intimations of an enduring reality. "Spiritual" is not synonymous with "religious"; all areas of the curriculum may contribute to a pupil's spiritual development.[13]

Here no reference is made to the religious realm. The question has been raised whether it is really possible to be spiritual without being religious. In a contemporary context this is certainly so—this is also an aspect of postmodernity. But there can be no doubt that education toward greater awareness is needed for all people to discover this spiritual potential within themselves. As has been rightly said, "very, very few people will become accomplished in the spiritual life without studying it in some way, whether theoretical or practical."[14]

In the past, such education for spirituality was always given in the context of one particular faith, within the definite social and institutional setting of a particular religious tradition. Spirituality was lived experience; it was a praxis that became formulated in particular teachings, as spiritual disciplines and counsels of perfection, that could guide others in turn on the path to holiness. But this holiness was not always *wholeness*, in the sense in which we understand it today as the integral development of the whole human person in balanced relationship with others, embedded in community. It often was very one-sided, antisocial and especially antiwoman.

Much spirituality in the past was developed by a social, cultural and intellectual *male* elite. A comparative study of the counsels of holiness and perfection in different religions reveals that the spiritual search of men was often related to their contempt for the body and the world. Frequently this included a specific contempt for women. Yet in spite of the most difficult conditions and obstacles, women have struggled throughout the ages to follow their own spiritual quest. The world history of renunciation and asceticism, which remains to be written, is certainly responsible for a great deal of misogyny. Much spirituality of the past can be seen as deeply dualistic in dividing men from women and men from each other and the world, and in separating too sharply the experience of the body, work and matter from that of the spirit. Much of spirituality was entirely *unwholesome.*

So how are we to assess the current interest in spirituality, the availability of "spiritual classics" of Christianity and other religions for the general reader, the efforts to promote the spiritual development of pupils?

Much critical thinking and debate are needed here, for a *simple revival* of past spiritualities is not enough. It could even be harmful. The *old agendas of spirituality* were too prescriptive, too much embedded in an ascetic and mystical flight from the world, too much centered on self-denial, which could be self-destructive rather than a path to real growth and fuller being. They were also too much tied to particular institutional settings and prescriptive, normative teachings, too much wedded to particular theological doctrines. A *merely historical approach* to studying different forms of spiritual life in the past, or a *theological approach* where the teaching of spirituality is tied to particular doctrines, is not sufficient for the development of the spirituality we need today. Critics have rightly pointed out that Christian spirituality has often been tied to an unhealthy ideology of obedience and suffering.

The current interest in spirituality parallels the modern emphasis on the subject, on individual self-development and the growth of a more differentiated understanding of human psychology. The contemporary *anthropological approach* to spirituality emphasizes that spirituality is intrinsic to the human subject as such. It is an approach that facilitates the resurgence and renewal of spirituality within a secular context. But one must ask then whether such an inclusive, universalizing understanding of spirituality gives enough attention to the social and political dimension of the human being in its definition of the human.

Christianity has always had a strong emphasis on the communal dimension, whether understood as the worshiping community, or the institution of the church, or the communion of saints, the body of Christ or the Kingdom of God. Yet much of traditional spirituality has been very individualistic in stressing the search of the soul for God. In medieval times the predominant locus of sanctification, where the spiritual ideal could be lived to the full, was the monastery, the convent, the cloister, which represented a parallel community separated from mainstream society. With the rise of Protestantism the place of sanctification shifted from the cloister to ordinary life in society with its day-to-day relationships and responsibilities. Thus at the beginning of the modern period a new *spirituality-of-being-in-the-world* developed, which was not without earlier parallels, but could now flower in new forms. Soon the tension, and even conflict, between religion and science developed. Contemporary sensibility still wrestles with this important issue—the challenge posed by the knowledge and world view of the sciences, our knowledge of the world around us and of ourselves.

Our knowledge has expanded at an exponential rate. Our world is marked by extraordinary pluralism, by dynamic change and movement, where traditional norms and values have been eroded. Nothing can any longer be taken for granted. We have to ask searching questions about the place of religion in the world today. Among Christians in the West churches are mostly empty, and the great credibility gap that opened up with modernity seems forever widening. Yet there are so many among both young and old who seek for greater fullness of life, for a new kind of wholeness that heals, empowers and reconnects us with all levels of contemporary life and experience. How can we find wholeness in body, heart, mind and soul? How can we construct a new kind of holiness, not the old, heroic type, but one linked to our ordinary day-to-day experience?

New ideas of embodiment, of transformation and integration, of inclusiveness of language and praxis, of the re-imagining and renaming of Ultimate Reality, abound. And so does a growing sense of the interdependence and sacredness of all life, and of our special human relationship to the whole earth and the cosmos.

To develop a *holistic, integral spirituality* that can respond to our new situation demands creative and critical rethinking of our traditions. Too often spirituality has been understood as a solid, reassuring fortress, clearly demarcated by the boundaries of tradition, narrowly defined and unchanging. But it is much more helpful to approach spirituality through the image of the journey, as something to be explored and ventured, as a process of growth and transformation. These processes have assumed new meanings in our contemporary context, but for Christians they link up with foundational narratives of the Hebrew and Christian scriptures, which speak of the journey of the exodus, the "walking according to the Spirit" described by St. Paul in Romans 8:4, the "way" followed by the early Christians in the Acts of the Apostles.

There is much we can relate to in the spiritualities of the past. They can awaken and inspire us, but they also need to be reformed and reformulated. Faced with the choice of so many different spiritualities, what can Christian spirituality offer us today? What is most distinctive about the Christian faith? What is its heart and center? And what keeps the flame of its spirit burning? Many contemporary Christian writers ask these questions, but they answer them quite differently. Teilhard de Chardin is rarely mentioned in contemporary discussions about Christian spirituality.[15] This is not only regrettable but a great loss, since there are few whose spirituality possesses such strength and power, such concrete embodiment coupled with such visionary qualities. His Christian faith led him to a deeply spiritual view of both creation and incarnation, with a strong affirmation and celebration of all life. His spiritual vision is both thoroughly traditional and utterly new and original. What was this vision, and what can it contribute to Christian spirituality today?

Why Is Teilhard's Thought of Great Significance for Christian Spirituality Today?

Teilhard de Chardin's life, spanning from 1881 to 1955, was one of passionate intellectual and spiritual adventure. He was certainly one of those human beings "in whom the soul of their age burnt *most intensely*."[16] Steeped in the world view of modern science as reflected in the disciplines in which he worked, geology and paleontology, but also biology, he produced in both his life and his work one of the strongest affirmations of the Christian faith in the incarnation. He celebrated the presence of God in all things through Christ. For him this was a presence strongly felt, fervently believed in and portrayed with a spiritual power rarely matched by other writers.

Yet for many people Teilhard is too complex, too difficult a writer, too daring an innovator. The power of his intellectual synthesis and spiritual vision is not always fully understood. The energizing resources of his life-affirming and life-celebrating spirituality are little drawn upon. The Christian churches have rarely recognized the contagious power of his Christian faith, a faith that was absolutely central to his vision and work. Yet Teilhard could say that he, like everybody else, walked in the shadows of faith, and that believing is not seeing. With rare insight he diagnosed the pulse of the modern world and asked where its frantic activity is going, what its ultimate goal is. He felt that today more than ever before it is imperative to feed the love for life, to maintain *"le goût de vivre,"* the zest for life that sustains individuals and communities. For this we need to discover the value of our work and efforts, strengthen the bonds of the human community through the powers of love and collaboration, find new models of holiness, and seek a new spirituality, a mysticism of action, that is truly commensurate to the world we know today.

Teilhard wrote a great deal about Christian spirituality. He also lived it. He is a marvelous embodiment and an inspiring example of Christian spirituality in the contemporary world. We find in him both a creative tension and synthesis of reason and faith, science and religion, rationality and mysticism. These elements are mirrored in his background, for on the one hand, through his mother's line, he was related to Voltaire, that passionate rationalist and critic of religion, and on the other hand he came from the same region of the Auvergne as Pascal, that passionate mystic full of the fire of faith, who three hundred years before Teilhard addressed the believers and scientists of *his* age and whose spirituality, like that of Teilhard, centered on the person of Christ. Other parallels can be drawn between these two men. When Teilhard died on Easter Sunday 1955 in New York, those who saw him then spoke of his face bearing "a striking resemblance to that of his compatriot from Clermont, Pascal:

the smooth forehead, the sunken cheeks, the prominent nose and cheek-bones, the tightly drawn lips."[17]

When Teilhard was studying theology at the beginning of the present century, he and his friends speculated about their future tasks. It was then that Teilhard was cast by his friends in the role of "apostle to the gentiles." More than ten years later, when he began to write during the First World War, he himself understood his vocation as that of an "apostle of Christ in the universe," an apostle called on the "road of fire." It was then that his mature spirituality was being forged and became marked by several striking characteristics. It could be described as the spirituality of a *pilgrim*, of someone always on the "road," on the move, of a wanderer between different worlds; as the spirituality of a *faithful servant* of God who persevered in his search and struggles until the end of his life; and as the spirituality of a *prophet and suffering servant* who experienced the depths of suffering and pain. These different aspects are best summed up in his motto "communion with God through the world."[18] To "communicate with all becoming" was his favorite formula.[19]

Teilhard's personal spirituality consisted in seeing all things in Christ, and Christ in all things. Christ was for him Alpha and Omega, the beginning and fulfillment of all created being. This is a very ancient Christian theme, deeply rooted in St. Paul and St. John's gospel, which Teilhard loved to contemplate and in which he had been steeped during this theological training. But like Pascal and others before him, Teilhard tried to translate these words into a new context and language in order to make them meaningful for people today. "Seeing" was the specific sense, almost the particular method, through which he achieved this translation and transformation, and it was through the repeated emphasis on the need to develop a special kind of seeing that he tried to convey his message.

"Seeing" in the Teilhardian sense is a process that implies "seeing more" and also "seeing differently," looking at the world from a different perspective in order to attain a larger vision, a new consciousness, a fuller life. To "see all things," especially to see all things in God, as is part of the Ignatian tradition to which Teilhard belongs, can no longer be taken as a straightforward descriptive statement. The mention of "all things" means so much more today than in the past. Our detailed scientific knowledge provides so much more detail and precision about *all* things. Now that we have discovered how to see the *infinitely small* and the *infinitely large,* Teilhard stressed the need to learn to see another, third dimension, the *infinitely complex,* which affects the interstructuring of *all things,* of all events, people, processes and relationships. In and through all things we can trace the process of growth, development and transformation. How can a Christian today still see all these things in and through Christ? As Teilhard rightly said, "If the world is becoming so dauntingly vast and powerful, it must follow that Christ is very much greater even than we used to think."[20]

How can the dynamic, living presence and energy of God be seen and encountered through the myriad things we know and meet today? That was Teilhard's question. For him God was found through all of life, through its warmth, its radiance, its power, its energy and its beauty, which he described with great lyricism. But divine life is also encountered through diminishment and decay, through death, suffering and pain, all of which Teilhard metaphorically called "the hands of God." These shape the experience of our life, with all its peaks and valleys, its activities and passivities. It was from this perspective that he spoke of the spiritual energy that can be drawn even from suffering. He certainly drew from it great strength, as can be seen from his experience in the trenches of the First World War when he began to say his "mass upon things" by offering up everything to God. As he wrote later, in 1923:

> In a sense the true substance to be consecrated each day is the world's development during that day—the bread symbolizing appropriately what creation succeeds in producing, the wine (blood) what creation causes to be lost in exhaustion and suffering in the course of its effort.[21]

He then wrote, "The more I look into myself the more I find myself possessed by the conviction that it is only the science of Christ running through all things, that is the true mystical science, that really matters."[22]

For Teilhard the figure of Christ was writ large on the universe, a universe he studied as a scientist. This is the way he saw it, but it is a vision that can be understood and makes sense only from within the Christian faith. But what could faith in Christ and christological doctrines possibly mean today if new horizons "were not opening up for our modern way of understanding and worshipping"?[23] In his essay "My Fundamental Vision" (1948), whose French title "Comment Je Vois" literally means "how I see," he expresses his own, new vision as a synthesis of "physics, metaphysics and mysticism." On reading it, one realizes that this vision is based on a powerful integration of science, religion and mysticism. It is this integral vision and synthesis that he wanted to transmit to others, as he said in a prefatory comment to that essay and again and again in many of his writings: "It seems to me that a whole life-time of continual hard work would be as nothing to me, if only I could, just for one moment, give a true picture of what I see."[24]

In the following chapters I present what Teilhard saw. I hope to show that he was empowered and fired by a dynamic spirituality of love and union, centered on a deeply incarnational and sacramental understanding of the world that was focused on seeing Christ in all things. I also hope to convince the reader that Teilhard's thought contains many seeds for Christian renewal today.

Chapter 2 examines the significant stages in *Teilhard's own spiritual experience,* which he often likened to the transforming energy and light of fire. Chapter 3 looks at *his writings on spirituality*, followed by a discussion of *his understanding of Christ* in Chapter 4. I then consider in Chapter 5 how Teilhard's *"new mysticism"* represents a new, holistic spirituality that possesses a great transformative potential for our world and bears witness to the empowering strength of the Christian faith.

The three remaining chapters look at spirituality in different contemporary contexts. I have chosen to explore several perspectives: those of religious pluralism and interfaith dialogue; of third-world women and theologians; of reflections on planet earth and new environmental concerns. All these themes are prefigured in Teilhard's thought and can be related to key elements in his own spirituality. His work provides one of the richest sources I know for finding a wholeness of vision of life on earth, and for living a new holiness in a world where the presence of God is encountered in the joys and sufferings of our ordinary day-to-day lives, blessed and transformed by the inexhaustible mystery of divine love and glory.

To conclude this first chapter, I would like to quote a prayer written by Teilhard and addressed to God in Christ. It is an integral part of his first essay, "Cosmic Life," written in 1916:

You the Centre at which all things meet and which stretches out over all things so as to draw them back into itself: I love you for the extensions of your body and soul to the farthest corners of creation through grace, through life, and through matter.

Lord Jesus, you who are as gentle as the human heart, as fiery as the forces of nature, as intimate as life itself, you in whom I can melt away and with whom I must have mastery and freedom, I love you as a world, as *this* world which has captivated my heart . . .

Lord Jesus, you are the centre towards which all things are moving: if it be possible, make a place for us all in the company of those elect and holy ones whom your loving care has liberated one by one from the chaos of our present existence and who now are being slowly incorporated into you in the unity of the new earth.[25]

CHAPTER TWO

"Rediscovering Fire"

The Power of Teilhard de Chardin's Spiritual Vision

ᏰᎿᎿᏰ

Teilhard de Chardin was certainly one of those human be-ings "in whom the soul of their age burnt *most intensely*,"[1] to repeat his own words once more. He was a man who glowed "with the fire divine," as a well-known hymn puts it.[2] The extraordinary intensity of his spiritual vision can best be summed up by the image of fire—a fire that meant to him the power of the Spirit, the presence of Christ and the all-trans-forming power of love. He thought that if humanity could learn to develop the powers of love to their highest, fullest extent, it would be like rediscovering fire. He expressed this in the much quoted phrase: "The day will come when, after harnessing the ether, the winds, the tides, gravitation, we shall harness for God the energies of love. And, on that day, for the second time in the history of the world, the human being will have discovered fire."[3]

Teilhard was such a "spirit of fire" that I chose this de-scription as the title for a new biography of him.[4] In one of his early essays he wrote of a friend—probably referring to him-self—that "his heart consumed him with fire within."[5] He described his own vocation as that of someone "whom the Lord had drawn to follow the road of fire."[6] This was early in his career, in 1919, when he had been ordained for eight years, more than half of which were spent in the trenches of the First World War. Toward the end of his life he could still say that he was full of a fire that consumed his heart and mind, that he retained the glorious vision of a world caught by the blazing fire of divine energy and love. It is not surprising, therefore, that he prefaced his spiritual autobiography, "The Heart of Matter" with the words "The Burning Bush."[7]

To discover something of the contagious power of Teilhard's spiritual vision and its significance for Christian spirituality today we must ask in what sense Teilhard was a true spirit of fire, and what is meant by the symbolism of fire.

In What Sense Was Teilhard a True Spirit of Fire?

Teilhard's ideas are highly nuanced and complex, but they focus on one single and compelling vision, that of the reassuring, radiant presence, the intimate nearness of God in all creation. More than his ideas and intellectual vision, it is the strength and power of his very vivid spirituality, the intensity of his experience and feeling, the fervent nature of his prayer and dedication to God, that can move our hearts and minds. Nowhere is the intensity of Teilhard's vision more strongly expressed than in his autobiographical essay, "The Heart of Matter," written in 1950 to trace the line of his inner, spiritual development. It is the key to his entire work, but few know it, for it was published only in 1976,[8] long after the far better known *Phenomenon of Man*.

Teilhard saw the whole universe on fire with God's love. He fervently believed in the continuous outpouring of God's ever-present love, which runs through all of creation and animates the immense rhythm of life everywhere. The experiences of his own life were always closely interwoven with his thought so that both must be read and interpreted together. Teilhard's basic theme is the human ascent to the Spirit, and the continuous breakthrough of God's presence into the world of matter and flesh. Thus his vision was one of consuming fire, kindled by the radiant powers of love. It was a mystical vision deeply Christian in origin and orientation, yet it broke through the boundaries of the traditional orthodoxies of both science and religion and grew into a vision global in intent.

Many of Teilhard's works are difficult to understand because of numerous new words and unfamiliar concepts.

Teilhard is all too often dismissed as an abstract intellectual, irrelevant to the life of faith. In my view this is a great misunderstanding of what the man stands for. A daring intellectual he was, but not primarily a rationalist or a man of abstract ideas. He was rather a passionate, dynamic and organic thinker, a man with a depth and intensity of feeling that are rare, not a detached, cool theorist who constructs abstruse thoughts in his study. On the contrary, his ideas originated and grew in living contact with the world, especially the earth. As a scientist he pursued a professional career in the fields of geology and palaeontology, and was also close to biology. His work brought him into constant contact with a world of rocks and stones, fossils and bones, plants and animals. At the same time, he was in touch with many different places and people whose precious friendships he enjoyed. All of these provided him with the concrete, tangible "stuff of the universe," as he called it.

While he worked on his specimens in the laboratory and wrote scientific papers in his office, he created most of his religious and philosophical works in a more unusual setting, different from that of most other academic writers, frequently far removed from any library. The most formative experiences for the emergence of his vision were his three years' stay in Egypt, from 1905 to 1908, and the deep impression made on him by excursions into the desert, the extraordinary experience of the First World War devoted to over four years' ministry of healing and pastoral counsel and, equally important, his discovery of China and the vastness of the Asian continent.

His earliest works were written in the trenches of the First World War, in woods and farm houses, whenever there was a respite from battle. In later years he often composed the final version of his essays on long boat journeys between Asia, America and Europe, or during vacations in his family home in the Auvergne, without access to a library. This manner of working accounts for the absence of extensive references and footnotes in his works. Much of the background and sources of his thought is hidden in subtexts and careful detective work is required to discover their full significance.

The foundations for Teilhard's *scientific* interests were laid by his father, who fostered in his children a great curiosity in natural history and encouraged them to collect stones and rocks, an easy task in the volcanic setting of the Auvergne. At the same time, Teilhard's *religious* interests were nourished by his devout Catholic family at home and by his education at a Jesuit boarding school. But it was above all his mother— his *sainte maman*—to whom he owed the best in himself. Her deep personal religiosity and great love of the Christian mystics oriented the young Pierre early on toward reading the mystics. But he would probably not have done so had it not been for an innate mystical tendency, which he later described as a "passion for the Absolute," a "passion for the universal Real." He certainly was no ordinary child, but one endowed with an extraordinary passion, a special gift and grace that made him search relentlessly for something consistent, coherent, indestructible and utterly permanent—a focus, a divine center, a supreme person he could worship, adore and love. This deeply religious orientation is also evident from his very early vocation, first expressed at the age of sixteen, and followed through by entering the Jesuit order at eighteen.

Numerous passages in his writings express this ceaseless quest, this deepest inner call to seek perfection and union with God as his one and only goal. All his striving, all his efforts, relate to this—his vocation to become a Jesuit and priest, his efforts to meet the most demanding challenges of a brilliant scientific career, his aim to live to the full the life of a man of his time while, at the same time, living up to the highest ideals of a Christian life—demands he sometimes summed up as the search for a "new definition of holiness." Underlying all of this was the search for a profound, essential unity of all things. This is what he referred to as an "inextinguishible core of fire," radiant within him. In my view, Teilhard de Chardin is a great Christian mystic, one of the important mystics of our own time, but also one whose particular search and synthesis of integrating modern science with the Christian faith could occur only in the modern period.

Science and religion, together with spirituality and mysticism, are inextricably combined in the experiences of his own life, but they also figure prominently in his thought. He assigned to them a decisive position in the further development of human evolution and of what it means to be fully human. Already in 1918 he could say about his own work:

> It seems to me that every effort I have made, even when directed to a purely natural object, has always been a religious effort: substantially, it has been one single effort. At all times, and in all I have done, I am conscious that my aim has been to attain the Absolute. I would never, I believe, have had the courage to busy myself for the sake of any other end.
>
> Science (which means all form of human activity) and Religion have always been for me one and the same thing; both have been, so far as I have been concerned, the pursuit of one and the same Object.[9]

For Teilhard the universe is not simply an object of scientific enquiry; it is a concretely experienced, living reality, a world he passionately loved and embraced as something alive, throbbing and pulsating with energy and growth. He refers to "Mother Earth," the *Terra Mater,* who is our matrix and ground, the "world-womb"[10] from which we grow and in which we have lasting roots, an earth whose immensity, richness and diversity of life he approached with deep reverence and a continuing sense of wonder. To comprehend his vision of the world, one has to be attuned to the tonality of his feeling, expressed through the metaphors of fire and music he so often used, speaking about a note, a melody, a sound, a rhythm that beats at the heart of the universe—or the spark, the glow, the leaping up of a flame, the blaze of fire that sets alight and consumes. He summed up this vision when he wrote:

> Throughout *my* life, by means of *my whole* life, the world has little by little caught fire in my sight until, aflame all around me, it has become almost luminous from within . . . Such has been my experience in contact with the earth—the diaphany of the Divine at the heart of the universe on fire.[11]

Later in the same essay he speaks of Christ as a fire capable of penetrating everywhere and gradually spreading everywhere.[12] It is in a blaze of fire and light that he saw Christ in all things. But what is the meaning of this fire? What does Teilhard associate with this metaphor he so frequently uses?

How to Understand the Symbolism of Fire

The fire metaphor is so all-pervasive in Teilhard's work that it invites special attention. The French philosopher Gaston Bachelard devoted a whole study to *The Psychoanalysis of Fire*[13] where he links the vital intensity of fire to the intensity of being, to the whole creative process of the imagination and the work of the poet. "Imagination works at the summit of the mind like a flame,"[14] Bachelard wrote. That is a quotation Teilhard would have loved.

Let us reflect for a moment on the significance of fire as a central element in the development of human life and culture. At the level of natural symbolism, fire is one of the four basic elements, besides earth, water and air. Fire is not organic like plants; it has neither roots, nor seeds, nor fruits, but appears as a fleeting, ephemeral, mysterious or even miraculous occurrence. Today many find it difficult to make the imaginative leap back into the far distant past, to the first discovery and use of fire, so much celebrated in myth and legend, and so important for ritual and cult. How can we ever recapture the fascination and spell that fire held for human beings at the dawn of history? Perhaps we can observe some of the magic of this attraction in the way small children are drawn to playing with fire.

The first discovery of fire and the harnessing of its use was a great step forward in the history of human civilization. As far as I know, Peking Man, whose fossils were found from 1929 onward and date to approximately 450,000 BCE, is said to have been the earliest unquestionable user of fire in human history.

The significance of this association between early Peking Man and fire cannot have been lost on Teilhard, for he was associated with the excavations at Chou Kou Tien near Peking, where the fossil bones of Peking Man were found together with cinders. It was in fact Teilhard himself who took these cinders to Europe to have them analyzed so as to establish the authenticity of this early human culture. And it was not long after finding the location of this first use of fire that Teilhard wrote the passage about discovering fire for a second time quoted at the beginning of this chapter. Bachelard has stated:

> We are almost certain that fire is precisely the first object, the *first phenomenon*, on which the human mind *reflected;* among all phenomena, fire alone is sufficiently prized by prehistoric man to wake in him the desire for knowledge, and this mainly because it accompanies the desire for love.

And also:

> The conquest of the superfluous gives us a greater spiritual excitement than the conquest of the necessary. Man is a creation of desire, not a creation of need.[15]

We feel this desire, this yearning, this search in Teilhard most vividly. Fire has been a central element of human life, important for the development of agriculture, pottery-making and metal smelting. It is an important sacred symbol in many religions of the world, for fire is associated with life, immortality and energy. And fire images have led to enormous poetic production, playing on the power of the dialectic of fire. Fire can both purify *and* destroy; human beings can give themselves to fire *and* be consumed by it. In the Hebrew Bible some of the best known references to fire are the burning bush, symbolizing Moses' encounter with God, and Elijah's ascent to heaven in a chariot of fire—both images Teilhard appropriated in his writings, and both events of great symbolic significance in the history of Jewish and Christian mysticism.

Teilhard's frequent recourse to images associated with fire shows the depth of his commitment and feeling, the intensity of his longing, the passionate power of his love. From the very first of his writings he wanted to communicate "the fire of his vision." What was this fire? How was it ignited and kept alight during the darkness and trials of life? What does he mean by the fire of love being a transforming energy that will bring us to God? And how can we catch something of Teilhard's fire? To answer these questions, we must discover how his own vision of fire was first brought into being.

The First World War: Teilhard's Baptism of Fire

Teilhard felt inspired and compelled to begin his writing amid the battle fires of the First World War. Almost daily at the boundary between life and death, he sensed the urgency of writing down his inner vision, for he felt he had seen something new that he wanted to pass on to others.

The war meant much more than battles, dangers and hardship to him. It was the discovery of a rich "human milieu," of the diversity of soldiers at the front drawn from very different backgrounds and countries, from many parts of the French colonies of that time. This was a vastly different, far more complex humanity than what he had experienced before in the sheltered setting of his family and religious life. The amount of work he completed in the exhausting conditions of battle is truly astonishing. With heightened sensibility and, some might say, extraordinary detachment, he went for lonely walks between battles and reflected on these questions: What was the meaning of life? Where was God on these fields of death and battle? What was humanity heading for? How did all these diverse human groups on both sides of the battle line, drawn not only from France and Germany but also from colonial territories in Africa and Asia, belong to one human family? What was the role of the Christian faith in the immense cosmic process that is the evolution of life?

Moved by such questions, Teilhard started a war journal; made notes; wrote letters to relatives and friends and composed a series of stirring essays. He wrote them for himself, but he also wrote them for the world, for he wanted to make others see what he felt, saw and believed. The real problem of his interior life was how to reconcile progress and detachment, how to combine a passionate and legitimate love of the earth's highest development with an equally passionate quest for the Kingdom of God.

During the war his life was bound up with the lives of many

other people, Christians, Muslims, atheists. Though an ordained priest, he had chosen to work not as a chaplain but as a stretcher bearer at the front. The North African Muslim soldiers of his regiment had no chaplain of their own; thus it was Teilhard who frequently assisted them in their dying moments. The Muslim soldiers acknowledged Teilhard's spiritual power by calling him *Sidi Marabout*, a North African term referring to a man closely bound to God, a saint and ascetic protected by *baraka* or divine power and grace, which, they believed, kept him invulnerable in all battles.

It was this daily closeness with people of different races and cultures which heightened Teilhard's sense of the organic unity of the human species. He was convinced that we are connected by all the fibers of our being—material, organic, psychic and mental—with everthing else around us. The human being, like every other being, is essentially cosmic. But all human beings together are in the process of forming a new and higher unity than merely that of a collection of individuals. It was amid the divisions of war that he first perceived this greater unity of humankind and began to think about how our humanness is invisibly but powerfully enhanced in the sphere of thought and love. He could see that the human world was a vast reality that, like a living organism, covers the entire globe. He called this vision first the rise of an immense "Thing," a unified, new earth, symbolized by the image of the moon rising over the trenches. From 1925 on he came to call this reality the "noosphere," a concept that occupies a central place in his thinking. He sees it suffused by the fire of the Spirit and fired by the powers of love.

Confronted with the possibility of a sudden death in the trenches, Teilhard felt a deep desire to leave his "intellectual testament" in case he did not return from the front. In the early months of 1916, he wrote with a great sense of urgency the first of his essays, soon to be followed by many more. They all express his love for the world, for all of life, but also his great love of God, seen as Christ present in all things. The beautiful lyricism and prayerful passages of these strongly autobiographical early essays express his mystic bent in a fresh and original way that his later works do not always recapture.

The first essay, entitled "Cosmic Life," recalls the ensorcelling appeal of nature, of life in the cosmos. He describes his own intoxication with the "temptation of matter" experienced in the haunting beauty of the desert, the sea, the woods charged with life, as he had encountered them when collecting rocks and fossils during his years in Egypt, Jersey, and Sussex. Should he abandon himself to this appeal of nature and surrender to matter? Become a pantheist, a monist?

That would have meant taking a wrong road of fusion and abandonment, whereas he was searching for something greater, more universal and transcendent, a reality that could incorporate all these experiences. He then made the ecstatic discovery that the whole of nature—matter, energy and life— was filled with divine energy and presence. He had moved, so to speak, from the material to the ultramaterial, and from there to the ultraliving and spiritual. In the evolutionary process of life he discovered the rhythm and breath of Spirit, the lineaments of the face and hands of God, the taking shape of what he called a universal being and what he recognized as God incarnate, present in the stream of becoming as a "christic" element in all things. This is Christ in the cosmos, whom he later named the "God-of-evolution," the universal Christ and "Christ-Omega."

"Cosmic Life" is preceded by the motto "To *Terra Mater,* and through her, above all, to Christ Jesus." It is in and through mother earth, through the life of nature and the world, that incarnate, divine life is encountered and felt in its full dimension. That is why the essay is preceded by the affirmation "There is a communion with God, and a communion with earth, and a communion with God through earth."[16]

The essay is signed Dunkirk, Easter week, April 1916. In the midst of terrible battles, surrounded by the experience of death, Teilhard opens with a great and extraordinary affirmation:

> I am writing these lines from an exuberance of life and a yearning to live; they are written to express an impassioned vision of the earth, and in an attempt to find a solution for the doubts that beset my action—because I love the universe, its energies, its secrets, and its hopes,

and because at the same time I am dedicated to God, the
only Origin, the only Issue and the only Term. I want to
express my love of matter and life, and to reconcile it, if
possible, with the unique adoration of the only absolute
and definitive Godhead.[17]

In the same essay he wrote:

God is at work within life. He helps it, raises it up, gives
it the impulse that drives it along, the appetite that
attracts it, the growth that transforms it. I can feel God,
touch Him, "live" Him in the deep biological current that
runs through my soul and carries it with it.

God shines through and is personified in mankind. It
is He to whom I lend a hand in the person of my fellow-
man; it is His voice I hear when orders come to me from
those who have authority over me . . .

The deeper I descend in myself, the more I find God at
the heart of my being; the more I multiply the links that
attach me to things, the more closely does He hold me—
the God who pursues in me the task, as endless as the
whole sum of centuries, of the Incarnation of his Son.[18]

And the essay ends with the words:

To live the cosmic life is to live dominated by the consciousness that one is an atom in the body of the mystical
and cosmic Christ. The man who so lives dismisses as
irrelevant a host of preoccupations that absorb the
interest of other men: his life is projected further, and his
heart more widely receptive.

There you have my intellectual testament.[19]

This essay is an affirmation and praise of life in the midst of
war. Teilhard always maintained his trust in life, but was not
unaware of life's contradictions and tensions, and the difficulty of holding on to faith. Years later he wrote: "What an
absurd thing life is, looked at superficially: so absurd that
you feel yourself forced back on a stubborn, desperate, faith
in the reality and survival of the spirit. Otherwise—were there
no such thing as the spirit, I mean—we should have to be

idiots not to call off the whole human effort."[20]

Teilhard's understanding of life is an integral, holistic one. Life is not only affirmation and celebration but includes darkness and death, suffering and pain, immense efforts, tremendous waste and destruction—just like the war. The Great War was like a crucible of fire wherein all his previous experiences became fused together into one great mystical vision that compelled him to write, and write ever more.

Seeing Christ in all things as the "cosmic Christ" involves the whole cosmos in its tremendous process of evolution where all matter is dynamic energy, full of promise and potential. This was a powerful experience for Teilhard, one he explained again and again in many other essays. I shall quote here from only two, the lyrical stories "Christ in the World of Matter," written in 1916, and "The Priest," composed in 1918. Both express beautifully Teilhard's strong sacramental and eucharistic spirituality, which pervades so much of his writing.

"Christ in the World of Matter" carries the subtitle "Three Stories in the Style of Benson," which requires some explanation. Teilhard was much impressed by the conversion novels of Robert Hugh Benson (1871-1914), the son of E. W. Benson, Archbishop of Canterbury, who became a Catholic and wrote fervently about his faith. Teilhard's short sketches probably recount his own experience of seeing Christ, an experience that may rightly be called mystical. Contemplating a picture of Christ in a church, Teilhard suddenly saw a figure of cosmic dimension emanating outward—from the picture, from a monstrance and from a pyx—but above all from Christ's heart and from the consecrated host, so that "the entire universe was vibrant."[21] He depicts Christ's figure in considerable detail, the iridescence of his face, the appeal of his eyes, the power of his attraction. I quote a few passages here:

> Over the glorious depths of those eyes there passed in rainbow hues the reflection . . . of everything that has power to charm us, everything that has life . . . And the luminous simplicity of the fire which flashed from them changed . . . into an inexhaustible complexity wherein were gathered all the glances that have ever warmed and mirrored back a human heart . . . these eyes which at first

were so gentle and filled with pity that I thought my mother stood before me, became an instant later, like those of a woman, passionate and filled with the power to subdue . . . And then they changed again, and became filled with a noble, virile majesty, similar to that which one sees in the eyes of men of great courage or refinement or strength, but incomparably more lofty to behold . . .

Now while I was ardently gazing deep into the pupils of Christ's eyes, which had become abysses of fiery, fascinating life, suddenly I beheld rising up from the depths of those same eyes what seemed like a cloud, blurring and blending all that variety I have been describing to you. Little by little an extraordinary expression, of great intensity, spread over the diverse shades of meaning which the divine eyes revealed, first of all permeating them and then finally absorbing them all . . .

And I stood dumbfounded.

For this final expression, which had dominated and gathered up into itself all the others, was *indecipherable*. I simply could not tell whether it denoted an indescribable agony or a superabundance of triumphant joy. I only know that since that moment I thought I caught a glimpse of it once again—in the glance of a dying soldier.

In an instant my eyes were bedimmed with tears. [22]

Here he reminds us of the context of his experience—the war and his presence among soldiers. His own emotions are acknowledged, the recognition of both agony and joy is expressed, but above all the overwhelming sense of an ingathering of everything in Christ as center of all realities and all human experiences. When holding the host, he felt "that I was not holding the host at all but one or the other of the thousand entities which make up our lives: a suffering, a joy, a task, a friend to love or to console."[23]

The host in his hands is suddenly perceived as "the entire universe," a revelation that filled him with a "feeling of rapture"[24] and he felt he was losing himself in it. Thus he could say "I live at the heart of a single, unique Element, the Centre of the universe and present in each part of it: personal Love and cosmic Power."[25]

Later, after the war, he celebrated the divine presence in

the universe in his hymn on "The Spiritual Power of Matter," and later still he offered up the whole of creation as a cosmic offering to God in his "Mass on the World." In the essay "The Priest" he speaks of his experience of being "submerged in the tears and blood of a whole generation."[26] And yet he could pray:

> Since today, Lord, I your Priest have neither bread nor wine nor altar, I shall spread my hands over the whole universe and take its immensity as the matter of my sacrifice . . .
>
> The seething cauldron in which the activities of all living and cosmic substance are brewed together—is not that the bitter cup that you seek to sanctifiy? . . .
>
> You, my God, have given me the gift of discerning, beneath this surface incoherence, the living and deep-rooted unity that your grace has mercifully imposed on—instilled beneath—our hopeless plurality.
>
> Let creation repeat to itself again today, and tomorrow, and until the end of time, so long as the transformation has not run its full course, the divine saying: "This is my body."[27]

Teilhard's war writings present a mystical view of Christ as the soul and heart of the world, and the world as body of Christ. Teilhard's understanding of his vocation as a priest is a mystical and sacramental one that he also described as *"To promote*, in however small a degree, *the awakening of spirit* in the world, is *to offer the* incarnate *Word an increase of reality and consistence*: it is to allow his influence to increase in intensity around us."[28] His offering up of the entire world to God was also shaped by *profoundly pastoral* concerns in helping to alleviate the suffering and pain of his comrades and in strengthening the faith in the presence of God among all he met.

Teilhard's war essays show us how he worked out his spiritual practice during the First World War. Later he explained it in greater detail, and more systematically, in *Le Milieu Divin* which bears the subtitle "An Essay on the Interior Life." He writes there that from his perspective "the world is not merely an exercise-ground: it is *a work* to be carried through" in which all human activity and passivity are "integrally sanctified and divinized." From the perspective of faith he could say: "Whatever is done to us, it is Christ who does it, and, whatever we do, it is to Christ we do it."[29] But he was also aware what a grace such a vision is: "The perception of the divine omnipresence is essentially a seeing, a taste . . . It is a gift, like life itself, of which it is undoubtedly the supreme experiential perfection."[30] How blessed he was!

Yet his pastoral experience and intense interest in the scientific breakthroughs of his time made him critically aware of the growing credibility gap between the Christian gospel and modern culture. Already in 1918 he wrote:

> Judging by my own case, I would say that the great temptation of this century (and of the present moment) is (and will increasingly be) that we find the world of nature, of life, and of mankind greater, closer, more mysterious, more alive, than the God of Scripture.[31]

This is why he pleaded for a more organic reinterpretation of "the age-old rules of Christian asceticism and direction," why he reflected from the war years onward on how to preach the Christian faith to our present generation, marked by new sensibilities, by the presence of new knowledge and by new technological developments. How to convey an image of God large and dynamic enough to be commensurate with the dimensions of the universe known today? These questions and themes were to remain with him for the rest of his life. He continued to reflect on them until his death, discovering ever new perspectives.

Can we still catch something of the fire of Teilhard's vision? Can we share just a little of the intensity of his faith and love?

What Teilhard Can Contribute to the Renewal of Christian Spirituality

I have mainly spoken of Teilhard's own spiritual experience rather than his thought on spirituality, which forms the subject of the next chapter. It seems to me that the Christian faith he lived and about which he wrote so vividly and passionately possesses such contagious power and fortifying strength that his example should be much better known among our contemporaries. It was a faith based on a deep trust in life and its direction; it was a faith in the goodness and splendor of creation; it was also a faith in the tremendous challenge and responsibility of being human, a faith in the shared destiny of the human community. Above all, it was a faith grounded in and crowned by faith in God's incarnate presence in the world—an almost superhuman faith in clinging to the power of the Spirit and believing in the beauty and wholeness of a redeemed world whose promise remains with us in spite of all contrary experiences and events.

Teilhard's spirituality is world-affirming and holistic. It is deeply rooted in a sacramental view of the world, and is nourished by eucharistic devotion and practice. It is centered in a firm faith in the incarnation, but an incarnation greatly extended and strengthened rather than reduced in its meaning. Such faith produced a beautiful, mystical spirituality, developed not in retreat from, but through immersion in, the world.

It is important to realize that Teilhard objected to any kind of "spiritual dualism."[32] His passionate sense of the divine milieu sees "the flame of the divine Presence"[33] everywhere. Like St. Paul long ago, he did not seek to engage in metaphysics or apologetics, but wanted to speak to people in the marketplace, in the Agora, about the "God whom we try to apprehend by the groping of our lives—that self-same God is as pervasive and perceptible as the atmosphere in which we are bathed. He encompasses us on all sides, like the world itself." Teilhard rightly asked, "What prevents you, then, from enfolding Him in your arms? Only one thing: your inability *to see Him*."[34] For Teilhard, "God truly waits for us in things, unless indeed He advances to meet us."[35]

Teilhard presents us with a particular vision of the world and of faith born out of a synthesis of science and religion. But more than anything else he proclaims a spirituality fired by the power of love, a love that combines the love of the world with that of God. Teilhard dedicated his *Milieu Divin* "to those who love the world." He loved the earth and its

peoples, he loved his church and his order, and he was filled
with the fire of love for "the ever greater Christ."

The symbol of fire meant for him above all the warmth
and radiance of love and light, the energy to fuse and transform everything. Of course fire is ambivalent; it can destroy
as well as transform. In Teilhard's understanding it is the
transforming power of the energies of love that alone can create a true human community and provide it with its strongest bonds, so that we can live in justice and peace. The fire
of love may be the only energy capable of extinguishing the
threat of another fire, namely that of universal conflagration
and destruction. The fire of love is what is most specifically
human; it is central to the full emergence of the noosphere,
understood as a world that is transformed and made whole, a
world that can be holy.

Teilhard was fond of the word "holism," first coined by the
South African Jan Smuts in his book *Holism and Evolution*,
published in 1927.[36] Like Smuts, Teilhard approached all
phenomena from a holistic perspective. He wanted a science
that studied the whole human phenomenon, a study not only
carried on through the most refined analysis but comple-
mented by a larger synthesis. Following from such a study,
the human phenomenon also invites the systematic study of
the *phenomenon of thought* and *of love*, the careful investiga-
tion of the *phenomena of religion, spirituality* and even *mysticism.*

Teilhard criticized the traditional concept of love as too
static, too "spiritualized," too divorced from its cosmic roots,
from natural passion in which all love, including the love of
God, has its starting point. He spoke of "the transformation
of love" whereby love itself is undergoing a change of state
that we have to study as systematically as any other aspect
of the human phenomenon, for love not only makes possible
and deepens personal development, but is equally necessary
for the development of society. As he wrote in his essay "The
Grand Option":

> Love has always been carefully eliminated from realist
> and positivist concepts of the world; but sooner or later
> we shall have to acknowledge that it is the fundamental

impulse of Life, or, if you prefer, the one natural medium in which the rising course of evolution can proceed. With love omitted there is truly nothing ahead of us except the forbidding prospect of standardisation and enslavement—the doom of ants and termites. It is through love and within love that we must look for the deepening of our deepest self, in the life-giving coming together of humankind. Love is the free and imaginative outpouring of the spirit over all unexplored paths. It links those who love in bonds that unite but do not confound, causing them to discover in their mutual contact and exaltation capable, incomparably more than any arrogance of solitude, of arousing in the heart of their being all that they possess of uniqueness and creative power.[37]

Love is a fire both human and divine. In one of his early essays Teilhard expressed the hope that he might find in all created beings "the divine Fire which plays in them as though in purest crystal"[38] and in "The Mass on the World" and other mystical writings he calls on the divine fire to come down to earth and transform it. In the beginning there was not only the Word, but there was *"Power"* and "there was the *Fire*"[39]— fire that stands for all the energy and the presence of the Spirit in the universe.

If Christianity is centered on the mystery of the love of God, and if this love is meant to be universal, for all people, places and situations, then this love must relate to all our experiences, to both our "activities" and our "passivities," as Teilhard would say. Theologians have reflected on the mystery of this love, mystics have celebrated and praised it, but are scientists, as we know them today, open to the analysis of love? Is this possible? Is it necessary for understanding ourselves, for the completeness of the human project, to probe more deeply the powers of love in human life and community?

Such questions open up a whole range of critical perspectives. Is the "rediscovery of fire"—the analysis of the powerful and transformative energies of love—necessary and possible in the realm of the academy and in the larger context of our contemporary global situation? I simply pose this question but have no answer at present. Teilhard often asked new questions, but he did not always provide us with answers. His questions are an invitation to test the strength and lasting value of Christian spirituality, especially its power of love. They are an appeal and challenge to rediscover its fire, to renew its flame.

At the end of his *Phenomenon of Man* Teilhard writes about Christian love:

> Christian love is incomprehensible to those who have not experienced it. That the infinite and the intangible can be lovable, or that the human heart can beat with genuine charity for a fellow-being, seems impossible to many people I know—in fact almost monstrous. But whether it be founded on an illusion or not, how can we doubt that such a sentiment exists, and even in great intensity . . . Is it not a positive fact that thousands of mystics, for twenty centuries, have drawn from its flame a passionate fervour that outstrips by far in brightness and purity the urge and devotion of any human love? . . .
>
> Is it not a fact . . . that if the love of God were extinguished in the souls of the faithful, the enormous edifice of rites, of hierarchy and of doctrines that comprises the Church would instantly revert to the dust from which it rose?[40]

For Teilhard the fire of Christianity burnt most ardently in a mysticism of love and union centered on the love of God in Christ, but expressed and understood in a new way. What this new mysticism meant to him and how he saw Christ as cosmic, human and divine will be explained later, especially in Chapters 4 and 5. But he also greatly extended and universalized his understanding of love by saying that "the only human embrace capable of worthily enfolding the divine is that of all human beings opening their arms to call down and welcome the Fire. The only subject ultimately capable of mystical transfiguration is the whole of humankind forming a single body and a single soul in charity."[41] In his essay "The Spirit of the Earth" (1931)[42] this great vision of one world and one human community is once again strongly expressed. If we wish to extend rather than diminish our capacity of being human, we have to draw on the "incredible power of love," "the primal and universal psychic energy," "the most universal, the most tremendous and the most mysterious of the cosmic forces." For Teilhard, love is "a sacred reserve of energy; it is like the blood of spiritual evolution" through which we can develop the sense of the earth and "the miracle of a common soul" for the world.[43]

Rediscovering the fire by harnessing the powers of love means the transformation of the entire human community. Teilhard extends his mysticism of love to global dimensions and provides us with wholesome advice on spiritual practice, integrating all aspects of our outer and inner worlds. Speaking of Teilhard as a mystic it is not inappropriate to conclude with a comment on the Christian mystics made by Evelyn Underhill. She once said that the mystics "maintain that awestruck outlook towards the Infinite, and that warmly loving sense of God's indwelling grace, without which all religious institutions quickly become mechanical and cold." It is the mystics who show best what Christian spirituality can be and what contribution it can make to human corporate life. In her view it is through communion with the mystics that we "can realize the actuality of the world of the spirit, and even catch something of their fire."[44]

To understand Teilhard's integral vision of science, religion and mysticism, we need to catch something of this fire. As another writer has said, being human is really about "having fire, flair, a holy spark of inspiration."[45] With Teilhard we can discover fire a second time by taking up his thoughts about the power of love, "its fiery vigour," "its astonishing power to *transform* everything and *replace* everything." Is that not what we truly need today, and what Christian spirituality requires most for its creative renewal?

CHAPTER THREE

Spirituality and Evolution

Discovering Our Deepest Energy Resources

ᏬᏍᏍᎠ

We saw in the last chapter that Teilhard's spiritual vision is deeply rooted in the formative experiences of his life. He was *a spirit consumed by fire*,[1] a man who most of all wanted to communicate and share his deeply personal, mystical vision of the Christian faith rather than present formal theological arguments about its metaphysics and doctrines. I mentioned that the creation of his religious works occurred in somewhat unusual circumstances, outside traditional university settings and within the context of the life of a research scientist and explorer much affected by two world wars. Not many British theologians have engaged with Teilhard's vision and work or critically appropriated his key ideas. Donald MacKinnon belongs to the few who have commented on some of Teilhard's thought,[2] whereas Charles Raven contributed an excellent study, *Teilhard de Chardin: Scientist and Seer*, the first biography to introduce Teilhard to English readers.[3]

MacKinnon speaks of the spiritual significance of the *Milieu Divin*, which he describes as "an exercise of imagination and spiritual perception."[4] He underrates perhaps the theological importance of Teilhard's work although he admits that the important cosmological dimension of his thought and the cosmological significance of Christ's life and work are still too much neglected in theology today.[5]

This raises two questions about contemporary theology. First, how does theology relate to Christian life and experience? Second, what kind of theology is still possible and credible today? What sort of theology do we need to nurture and enhance Christian faith and experience, to renew and strengthen Christian spirituality in a world of growing doubt and uncertainty?

Theology and Spirituality

All too frequently theologians, in particular Western theologians trained in a formal academic setting, are engaged in displaying their habitual skills of formal reasoning without providing spiritual nourishment. Thus it is increasingly difficult for a theologically informed faith to be a true source of life and energy. The theologians follow long-established, disciplined intellectual practices but all too often these are constrained by provincialism, by a parochialism of vision and by an excessive logocentrism. Mircea Eliade once made the point that many new intellectual breakthroughs in the modern world occurred not in universities but outside them, through the cross-fertilization of minds and ideas drawn from different disciplines and backgrounds. New discoveries and syntheses are often born out of transdisciplinary encounters and the bold embrace of diverse elements hitherto kept apart. Such daring and imaginative re-visioning of transdisciplinary strength is certainly the hallmark of Teilhard's work, born within an unusual context of very diverse experiences, encounters and cultures. It would not be inappropriate to call his achievement a form of "contextual theology," to use a contemporary expression forged in different circumstances. It is significant that such contextual theology with its concerns for political and social liberation, for justice, peace and the integrity of creation, proves to be one of the most vibrant and lively forms of theology today. Much of this has developed outside formal academic settings, within and through the struggle of communities, especially in the so-called Third World. Such theology does nurture and enhance Christian life and witness and provides a context for some very strong "newly emerging spiritualities," which I will consider in a later chapter.

Some years ago Dorothy Emmet argued that theological

ideas were losing their impact because theologians were taking "refuge in studies of their past history but as present thought theology is high and dry, because it is no longer fed by the springs which used to feed it from science, philosophy and the mystical life." By contrast, *religious* interests and concerns are more alive than ever before, she maintained, and yet they are not met by the ways in which professional philosophers and theologians try to interpret them.[6] I do not think this statement applies to *all* theologies today, though it certainly applies to a great many. But it is contradicted by the existence of contextual theologies of various kinds. Yet the growth in religious interests and concerns and the existence of spiritual emptiness and hunger that are not adequately met by theologians are even more noticeable today than when Dorothy Emmet wrote this passage.

This highlights the fact that there exists not one, single theology but that theology too, like everything else, is affected by diversity and pluralism. Therefore we can only speak about theolog*ies* in the plural, although particular groups and institutions create their own, particular theology in the singular. The plurality of theologies in general is an indication of richness and strength rather than weakness; it is cause for celebration, not regret. It allows for more debate and for more voices to be heard.

Formal, systematic theology has been much too uniform, too exclusive of differences and too hierarchically dominant to cope with the pluralistic situation of the contemporary world whose sensibilities are often characterized as "postmodern." This can be understood as a critique of all false universalizations and unitary conceptions that have dominated all thought, not least theology. Such a critique is both necessary and welcome, but postmodernism as a contemporary intellectual trend is itself far too much characterized by fragmentary perspectives, which can easily lead to nihilism. When seen positively, postmodernism highlights the need for attention to the *particular* and *concrete*, to *individuality* and *difference*. It is here that one can see some of Teilhard's thought as definitely postmodern rather than modern. From such a perspective MacKinnon's distinction between *formal theology* and the *"theologically disciplined spirituality,"* which he sees as Teilhard's particular strength, appears artificial. But I would agree with his assessment that "Teilhard writes in the first instance to correct the philistine narrowness of vision, the gross deficiency of spiritual imagination, that he finds among the devout in their attitudes to the universe, and also to the majesty of the human mind's achievement in penetrating its secrets,"[7] even though this may not be the best way of expressing Teilhard's approach to consciousness and knowledge. Yet MacKinnon is right in saying that Teilhard invites the reader to follow him in an exercise of spiritual perception. Although this comment was made with special reference to the *Milieu Divin,* it can be equally applied to other writings of Teilhard, especially those on spirituality.

The powerful appeal of Teilhard's spiritual vision lies in the originality of his synthesis: It is a combination of a strong traditional Christian praxis with prophetic new ideas. Several writers have commented on this. David Tracy has said that Teilhard's understanding of spirituality in an evolutionary perspective "is one of the strongest affirmations of Catholic incarnationalism in the whole tradition . . . The immanence of God in all creation has rarely been portrayed with such spiritual power."[8] Teilhard's work discloses "a new envisionment of both traditional Catholic spirituality and scientific modernity in a manner that illuminates and transforms both."[9]

Thomas Corbishley opened his *The Spirituality of Teilhard de Chardin* with the bold statement: "The Teilhardian revolution—it is nothing less—in so much of our thinking finds its truest and most significant expression in the whole field of what we traditionally refer to as 'spirituality.' "[10] I wholly endorse Father Corbishley's view and wish to show why and how this is so, and why it can be said that "Teilhard built on traditional foundations to present to his contemporaries what can justly be described as a Faith for the Twentieth Century."[11]

To understand Teilhard's central concern with spirituality, we need to consider the connections between evolution and spirituality, between energy and spirituality, and also the role of spirituality, especially Christian spirituality, in the development of the earth and the human community.

Evolution and Spirituality

Let us first consider what Teilhard understands by spirituality, and why his view, though in many ways so traditionally orthodox, is nonetheless also revolutionary. The prime reason for this is the link he makes between evolution and spirituality. His is not a *philosophia perennis*, an unchanging, eternal, essentialist view of spirituality. No, spirituality is dynamic and transformative, part of an ongoing process of development and growth, of greater insight and fuller being. Like the Indian thinker Sri Aurobindo, who applied evolutionary insights to the reinterpretation of Hinduism, Teilhard maintained that evolution not only revolutionizes our attitude to the world and to ourselves, but also deeply transforms religion and spirituality.[12]

Teilhard often practiced what has been called "an extension of concepts." He stretches the meaning of concepts almost to their limit by combining different aspects not usually associated with a particular concept in order to express something new or express an idea differently, in a more nuanced and differentiated manner. This can greatly enrich our thinking, but can also lead to confusion and misunderstanding.

Such an extension of meaning is certainly evident in his use of the terms "evolution" and "phenomenon." A phenomenon is any kind of observable event or appearance with both exterior and interior aspects. The sciences have been particularly concerned with material, physical and organic phenomena, with their outside more than their internal organization. Teilhard sees the whole process of evolution as an immense cosmic event that affects matter, life and spirit, a process moving forward and upward toward greater complexity and consciousness. Creation is an ongoing process that continues to unfold through evolutionary development.

In contrast to Bergson's theory of creative evolution, understood as a movement of expansion and divergence, Teilhard spoke of *evolutionary creation* whereby an increasing process of centering and convergence is taking place in the world. He describes this as a process of "creative union"[13] whereby creation takes place continuously through the ongoing process of union, which has both an active and a passive form. Thus all created things are dipolar in structure, both active and passive; they are actively uniting or passively being united. *To be more* is to be united with a greater number of elements or to actively unite oneself with a greater number of others. This *theory of creative union* is also important for Teilhard's understanding of spirituality, where he always maintains a dynamic balance between activities and passivities, growth and diminishment.

In the human being evolution has become conscious of itself; it has become self-reflective so that thought and action can shape the further development of the world and of the human community. Teilhard reflected continuously on the human phenomenon—*le phénomène humain*. His most famous work on that subject was unfortunately in English given the title of *The Phenomenon of Man*. It is hoped that this work will soon be published in a new, poetically and linguistically more correct translation. Besides the human phenomenon, Teilhard also spoke of the religious and mystical phenomenon, the phenomenon of Christianity and the phenomenon of spirituality.

He argued that all these phenomena, even the most interior ones, ought to be studied from a strictly scientific point of view, with critical attention to detail. Although Teilhard sometimes either did not recognize or did not sufficiently acknowledge the growing dangers of modern science and the enormous ethical problems it has given rise to, of which we are much more aware today, he was not a positivist in affirming the strength of systematic, scientific research. He described the process of scientific analysis as an "admirable and powerful tool for dissecting the real"[14] but an insufficient one, because it leaves us with impoverished results, with a reduced view of the world. It is not only analysis we need, but synthesis, attention to the construction of the world through our consciousness and to the principle and presence of spirit.

In *The Phenomenon of Man* and again, more succinctly, in his subsequent book *Man's Place in Nature,* Teilhard describes the evolutionary process of becoming—from the stuff of the universe to the arising of life, of thought, of the human community and of a new "spirit of the earth" where further development occurs at the social, cultural and global levels. That is what the North American Catholic ecologist Father Thomas Berry means by the close relationship between the universe story and the human story, which in the final analysis is a story of the unfolding, birth and growth of spirit. He strongly endorses Teilhard's vision when he writes:

> From the viewpoint of our present understanding of the universe it could be said that Teilhard is the most significant Christian theologian since Saint Paul. The future efficacy of the Christian project will depend extensively on our capacity to understand Teilhard 1) in his understanding of the evolutionary process as having a psychic-spiritual as well as a material-physical dimension from the beginning; 2) in the intimate relation he establishes between the universe story and the human story, especially in the realm of spirituality; 3) in his shifting of our tendency toward an exclusive concern with redemption to a greater emphasis on creation.[15]

The process of evolution is a process of growing spiritualization through greater unification and complexity, through greater centering and convergence. From the perspective of faith it is a process that has its origin and end in God, in a final summit that Teilhard calls Point Omega or Christ-Omega. This Point Omega is a transcendent focus of convergence, conceived as both preexistent and transcendent. Teilhard's concept of God is close to the God of process theology and emergent evolution in that God is complete in Godself but appears to be growing for us. As is stated in the *Milieu Divin*:

> God does not offer Himself to our finite beings as a thing all complete and ready to be embraced. For us He is eternal discovery and eternal growth. The more we think we understand Him, the more He reveals Himself as otherwise. The more we think we hold Him, the further He withdraws, drawing us into the depths of Himself. The nearer we approach Him through all the efforts of nature and grace, the more He increases, in one

and the same movement, His attraction over our powers, and the receptivity of our powers to that divine attraction.[16]

Teilhard's enquiry embraces the development of the human phenomenon from its origins to its ultimate summit. The human being is rooted in nature, is part of the cosmic flux and creative transformation of matter into spirit. Thus evolution is ultimately an ongoing process of greater interiorization, of the growth of the spirit to its fullness and plenitude, so that evolution can also be described as a process of increasing spiritualization.

Some of Teilhard's critics consider this vision too large, too complex, too frightening or simply too fanciful, too poetic. They fear that the individual person might be lost in this vast process of evolutionary development. But for Teilhard there exists a dialectical relationship between growing personalization and increasing socialization, the centering of the human person and the strengthening of bonds between persons in the human community.[17] Not only are we affected by the geosphere, the biosphere, the atmosphere, but a new reality is born: the emergence of what he called the *noosphere*, a sphere of human thought and love, of knowing, acting and bonding that is increasingly covering all parts of the globe like an immense net or web with its own reality and decisive importance for the further development of the human community.

Teilhard enquired above all into what it means to be human today, at the end of the twentieth century on the threshold of a new era. What specifically singles out the *humanum* in the cosmic process of the evolution of life and consciousness, of which humankind is an integral part? The human being is not "the immobile centre of an already completed world," but "the extension and crowning point of *the living*," even "the most living part of life."[18]

In Teilhard's view the full development of the human phenomenon at the individual and collective level cannot be dissociated from the phenomenon of religion, the phenomenon of spirituality and the phenomenon of mysticism. He speaks far more often of mysticism than of spirituality, but he sometimes also uses these two words interchangeably, for at the heart of spirituality there exists for him a rightly understood mysticism. I will consider his specific understanding of mysticism in Chapter 5. Here I want to clarify the more general understanding of spirituality, which is closely connected with what he calls "the activation of energy" in the human being.

Energy and Spirituality

Scientists understand energy as a very specific force whose power can be calculated and measured. When speaking about energy, most of us are wont to think about material energy, but besides material and physical energy, human beings also need psychic and mental energy. They ultimately need spiritual energy. The concept of energy is absolutely central to an understanding of Teilhard's approach to spirituality, for he sees the religions of the world as an immense reservoir of spiritual energy resources without which we cannot build up the much needed greater unity and strength of the human community. But here again he considerably extends the meaning of a concept by using the word "energy" analogically.

For Teilhard energy has many different, yet interrelated meanings. In its simplest form energy is the capacity for action and interaction; it is a "unifying power" and for science today it represents "the most primitive form of the universal stuff."[19] Energy is thus another name for matter. Energy is pulsating throughout the universe; it is the basic driving force, the fundamental dynamism of all there is. Energy expresses itself in many forms—from the physico-chemical levels to biological and psychic centers. Cosmic energy organizes itself to form the living body, and material energy is increasingly used, controlled and manipulated by human beings through science and technology, more and more to the detriment of our environment.

At the human level, physical, mental and spiritual energy are most closely interwoven and integrated. These different forms of energy find their highest expression in love, which is human energy par excellence, its most noble form, an all-embracing transformative and creative principle. We need spiritual energy for action and collaboration, for growth and fulfillment. In 1937, during the same year that he wrote "The

Phenomenon of Spirituality"[20] Teilhard also wrote the essay "Human Energy." He also included the section "Spiritual Energy" in his book *The Phenomenon of Man,*[21] where he points out that because science has decidedly ignored the question of spiritual energy, this problem now urgently needs to be addressed. He writes:

> There is no concept more familiar to us than that of spiritual energy, yet there is none that is more opaque scientifically. On the one hand the objective reality of psychical effort and work is so well established that the whole of ethics rests on it and, on the other hand, the nature of this inner power is so intangible that the whole description of the universe in mechanical terms has had no need to take account of it, but has been successfully completed in deliberate disregard of its reality . . .
>
> What makes the crux . . . of the problem of spiritual energy for our reason is the heightened sense that we bear without ceasing in ourselves that our action seems at once to depend on, and yet to be independent of, material forces . . .
>
> "To think, we must eat." That blunt statement expresses a whole economy, and reveals, according to the way we look at it, either the tyranny of matter or its spiritual power. The loftiest speculation, the most burning love are, as we know only too well, accompanied and paid for by an expenditure of physical energy. Sometimes we need bread, sometimes wine, sometimes a drug or a hormone injection, sometimes the stimulation of a colour, sometimes the magic of a sound which goes in at our ears as a vibration and reaches our brains in the form of inspiration.
>
> Without the slightest doubt *there is something* through which material and spiritual energy hold together and are complementary. In the last analysis, *somehow or other*, there must be a single energy operating in the world.[22]

Toward the end of his life Teilhard dreamed of founding an "Institute of Human Energetics" to maintain and increase the "zest for life"—the *goût de vivre*—in the human community. For him the zest for life is the ultimate mainspring of evolution. At the human level, this zest or taste is absolutely necessary for the further development of human life. To recognize the need for feeding the zest for life, to acknowledge the indispensable role of spiritual energy in human development, invites special attention and reflection on the part of human beings. It calls for a new form of "praxis," to use a modern concept. In his essay "The Zest of Living" (1950), written after the Second World War, Teilhard pointed out that

> all over the earth the attention of thousands of engineers and economists is concentrated on the problem of the world resources of coal, oil or uranium—and yet nobody, on the other hand, bothers to carry out a survey of the zest for life: to take its "temperature", to feed it, to look after it, and (why not, indeed?) to increase it . . .
>
> In a world which has become conscious of its own self and provides its own motive force, what is most vitally necessary to the thinking earth is a faith—and a great faith—and ever more faith.[23]

He speaks of the *evolutionary role* of religions, of the "reserves of faith"[24] that contain spiritual energy resources on which the human community must draw to develop all its potential. Only then can it find its fulfillment in Point Omega, in God. A creative, holistic spirituality can draw spiritual energy out of all human experiences, out of activities and passivities, out of attachment and detachment, out of growth and diminishment, as is so beautifully described in *Milieu Divin*.

What does Teilhard then mean by spirituality? This is best explained in his essay "The Spiritual Phenomenon,"[25] written in 1937, but unfortunately little known.

The Spiritual Phenomenon

The rich resonances of Teilhard's understanding of spirituality—so much fuller, more concrete, cosmic, personal, social and holistic than the traditional, dualistic meaning of that word—can be captured only if one links the transformative potential and power of spirituality to what he called the "sense of man"—the sense of the human phenomenon and its zest for life—and to the sense of direction inherent in the evolution of life and its dynamic. For Teilhard the understanding of the fullness of life relates ultimately to fullness in Christ. The world must have a heart, a soul, a face—and from the perspective of the Christian faith this is the face of Christ.[26]

The meaning of spirituality is also related to what Teilhard called "the spirit of the earth," a vision of the whole planet expressed in a reflective essay of that title, written with great clarity and commitment in 1931 on one of his return journeys from China.[27] This work proclaims the sense of oneness, of the unity of the earth and all its peoples. It is a vision that first emerged for him in the trenches of the First World War. Subsequently, through his worldwide travels, this grew into the desire to write about the destiny of humanity as a whole, to write about it not as a Frenchman or a Westerner, but as a "terrestrian."[28]

In "The Spirit of the Earth" Teilhard links the future of the whole earth with the future of the spirit, with "the arising" rather than the eclipse or death of God. As so often, he affirms here the primacy of the spirit in the universe, the movement toward greater consciousness, as well as the "cosmic problem of action." He means by this that we have to meet the challenge to reflect on the values needed to decide on the right kind of action and the choices we have to make. We have to take full responsibility for the development of both the human community and further scientific research. What *is* the future of the spirit on earth? Teilhard maintained that humanity is presently undergoing a crisis of birth in which

> everything depends on the prompt emergence of a soul
> . . . this soul, if it exists, can only be the "conspiration" of
> individuals, associating to *raise* the edifice of life *to a new
> stage.* The resources at our disposal today, the powers
> that we have released, *could not possibly be absorbed* by
> the narrow system of individual or national units which
> the architects of the human earth have hitherto used . . .
> *The age of nations has passed. Now, unless we wish to
> perish we must shake off our old prejudices and build the
> earth* . . . The more scientifically I regard the world, *the*

*less can I see any possible biological future for it except
the active consciousness of its unity.* Life cannot henceforth advance on our planet . . . except by breaking down
the partitions which still divide human activity and
entrusting itself unhesitatingly to faith in the future.[29]

The spiritual phenomenon is just as real and natural as
are all the myriad phenomena studied by science. On one
hand Teilhard argues against spiritualist-idealist philosophies, and on the other he refutes all empirical-materialist
ones. The phenomenon of the spirit is neither an additional
nor simply a passing phenomenon; it is absolutely central
and integral to evolution. It has attracted human attention
more than any other: "We are coincidental with it. We feel it
from within . . . It is the thing we know best in the world
since we are itself." And yet spirit "seems so small and frail
. . . In face of the vast material energies to which it adds absolutely nothing that can be weighed or measured, the 'fact
of consciousness' can be regarded as negligible."[30]

For Teilhard, the true name for spirit is "spiritualization,"
understood as a process of unification, transformation and
convergence, a process that culminates in the union with God
or Christ-Omega. He writes:

As regards the final nature of the spirit into which all
spirituality converges . . . we see that its supreme sim-
plicity contains a prodigious complexity. In that spirit
. . . all the elements into which the personal consciousness of the world appeared in the beginning to be broken
up . . . are carried to their maximum individual differentiation by maximum union with the All and then extended without becoming confused with one another . . .

As regards the direction of our present activity, we
observe that, to complete ourselves, we must pass into a
greater than ourselves.[31]

Teilhard also asked how such a perspective affects our present
crisis in morality. He envisaged the way forward not through
the old "morality of balance" but through a "new morality of
movement." The moralist should not be a jurist who merely

tries to preserve the individual and the balance of society but rather aim to be "the technician and engineer of the spiritual energies of the world" whose task it is "to develop, by awakening and convergence, the individual riches of the earth"[32]

Such a morality of movement is seen as governed by three principles:

1. *Only* finally good is what makes for the growth of the spirit on earth.

2. Good (at least basically and partially) is *everything* that brings a spiritual growth to the world.

3. Finally *best* is what assures the highest development to the spiritual powers of the earth.[33]

Given Teilhard's scientific training, these ideas about the growth of the spirit and the presence of the spiritual phenomenon in the development of the world are put forward as a hypothesis, a theory. The hypothesis of a cosmos "in spiritual transformation"[34] seems best to explain all the features of the world. But beyond the explanatory power of this theory Teilhard sees further proof for it in the experience of the mystics and their love of God. He argues that "the definitive discovery of the phenomenon of the spirit is bound up with the analysis (which science will one day finally undertake) of the 'mystical phenomenon,' that is the love of God."[35] In other words, it is the fire of love that is "the most powerful, the most transformative and the most spiritualizing force on earth."[36]

But how can we activate such spiritual energy? How can we have access to it? Where do we find the deepest resources to develop our spirituality and feed its energy into our action and work?

Harnessing Resources for the Spirit

For Teilhard the human being remains incomplete without the development of the spiritual dimension. It is the spiritual that supplies the deepest energy resources for human beings, but the spiritual is rooted in and closely interwoven with the material, the physical, with our embodiment, our sexuality, our interpersonal relationships, our social structures. How to develop the spiritual?

For religious believers the deepest spiritual resources are

found in their faith. For Teilhard it was certainly his strong Christian faith that inspired and energized him and carried him onward and forward through all the vicissitudes of his life. His book *Le Milieu Divin* is a practical treatise of spirituality that can help us to transform our vision and attitude by seeing all experiences from a spiritual point of view. The book is written from an orthodox Christian perspective but its advice is such that its insights can help everybody. It tells us how we can draw spiritual energies out of *all activities*, out of every endeavor. Similarly, we can be energized and draw spiritual nourishment and strength from *all passivities*—every disappointment and darkness, every loss and death, every diminishment can help us to grow and be transformed, if we but learn how to develop this transformative spiritual practice. Communion with the powers of the spirit, with a divine center we call God, can be practiced through both action and diminishment. For the Christian this means a process of divinization, a journey into God, not through separation from the world but through its development and transformation.

Thus Teilhard emphasizes the importance of the "sanctification of all human endeavour," but stresses at the same time the need for a "humanisation of Christian endeavour."[37] Do Christians often "not give grounds for the reproach of being, if not the 'enemies,' at least the 'stragglers' of the human race?" he asks. But how "could we be deserters, or sceptical about the future of the tangible world? How could we be repelled by human labour?" Yet he admits that "far too many Christians are insufficiently conscious of the . . . responsibilities of their lives, and live like other men, giving only half of themselves, never experiencing the spur or the intoxication of advancing God's Kingdom in every domain of humankind."[38] Teilhard wants to prolong the perspectives of human endeavor to infinity. Christianity should not paralyze human endeavor but be a "soul of immense power which bestows significance and beauty . . . on what we are already doing."[39] Even the symbol of the cross is seen as a sign of transformation rather than renunciation. Rightly understood, it is a tremendous source of spiritual power.

Nowhere is this made more explicit than in the essay "The Significance and Positive Value of Suffering,"[40] a short piece written at the request of his permanently ill, younger sister who edited a bulletin for the Catholic Union of the Sick. Here Teilhard points to the potential energy that can be drawn even out of the experience of weakness and pain. A world of growth, of development and motion, is sublimated and spiritualized not only through the contemplative and prayerful, but also by the sick and suffering if they themselves can assign a deeper significance to their pain. As Teilhard writes:

> Illness naturally tends to give sufferers the feeling that they are useless or even a burden on the earth. Almost inevitably they feel as if cast up by the great stream of life, lying by sheer ill-luck incapable of work or activity. Their state seems to have no meaning. It reduces them, they might say, to inaction amidst a universe in action . . .
>
> What a vast ocean of human suffering spreads over the entire earth at every moment! Of what is this mass formed? Of blackness, gaps and rejections? No, let me repeat, of potential energy. In suffering the ascending force of the world is concealed in a very intense form. The whole question is how to liberate it and give it a consciousness of its significance and potentialities . . . All the sufferers of the earth joining their sufferings so that the world's pain might become a great and unique act of consciousness, elevation and union. Would not this be one of the highest forms that the mysterious work of creation could take in our sight?[41]

This is looking at suffering from a spiritual perspective. It is not to belittle or condone suffering but to energize the sufferer, to empower those suffering to see significance in their affliction and draw strength from it. It is an enabling rather than a debilitating strategy that Teilhard recommends as counselor and pastor, deeply concerned to help and give meaning to situations that might initially provide more reason for depression and despair than for hope.[42]

To maintain and develop spiritual energies was Teilhard's continuing concern. Population and food problems, economics and politics, environmental issues and education, all are related to the need for spiritual energy. Teilhard refers to "the theory and experience of spiritual energy,"[43] which are absolutely necessary now that we have reached a decisive point in global human development where we are "inevitably approaching a new age," as he wrote in 1937.[44] At present, so much of human energy is devoted to destruction rather than greater unity, to the "most primitive and savage form of war" where we "manufacture ever greater and more destructive weapons," machines that "translate the vital sense of attack and victory into concrete experience. But may the moment come (and it will come) when the masses realize that the true human victories are those over the mysteries of matter and life."[45] If only we could develop the available human energies "to the levels of spiritualized energy,"[46] we could then bring forth and enlarge the love or sense of humanity. For Teilhard this is possible only through greater collaboration and convergence, through developing the powers of love so that "a maximum of physical power may coincide with a maximum of gentleness and goodness."[47]

He was optimistic, perhaps far too optimistic and not sufficiently realistic, in assessing the impact of global power politics, when he argued that the development of the atom bomb might lead to the elimination of war, that "the very excess of destructive power placed in our hands must render all armed conflict impossible" and lead to greater unity in the world. But he was right in believing that "the state of psychic disarray which the atomic shock has induced in us"[48] must sooner or later lead to a fundamental choice about the future of the human community, the question of how to live in peace on this planet. He spoke of the increase in leisure, the quantity of unused human energy that "is growing at a disturbing rate both within us and around us" and the *rise in boredom*, the great enemy number one. "Perhaps this is the underlying cause of all our troubles. We no longer know what to do with ourselves. Hence in social terms the disorderly turmoil of individuals pursuing conflicting and egoistical aims; and, on the national scale, the chaos of armed conflict in which, for want of a better object, the excess of accumulated energy is destructively released."[49]

Are we going to follow the spirit of force or the spirit of love? What road will humanity take? Christianity still has a powerful message about the spirit of love, the spirit of service and giving; it adores a God who is the source of all love, a burning fire that creates, transforms and redeems, a God whose vivifying energies run through all things. The ultimate energy is for Teilhard a "love-attraction": "God's love for the world and for each of its elements, and the elements' love, too, for one another and for God."[50] These are not an added, secondary effect but represent the fundamental dynamism of the whole creative process. He passionately believed in the power of love as a power of transformation for the whole human community, a power whose genesis as "a collective and unique action" moved by a single, common desire was a practical necessity rather than love being only a code of moral perfection, charity and human sympathy that we may or may not practice. It is no longer enough to love one another in order to be perfect but we have to add "Love one another or you perish." Teilhard was convinced that we have now *"reached a decisive point in human evolution, at which the only way forward is in the direction of a common passion,"* a love of all human beings for each other. For him this was not an idea of dreamers, but the realistic goal of practical minds: "Either we must doubt the value of everything around us, or we must utterly believe in the possibility, and I should now add in the inevitable consequences, of universal love."[51]

The development and current state of the world are not a reason for disbelief and loss of faith, but a new opportunity to explore the question of God and the role of faith from a fresh perspective. Growing consciousness in the world entails the growth of spirituality. In "The Spiritual Repercussions of the Atom Bomb"[52] (1946), Teilhard concluded that "the final effect of the light cast by the atomic fire into the spiritual depths of the earth is to illumine within them the over-riding question of the ultimate end of Evolution—that is to say, the problem of God."[53]

Today there exists a growing popular interest in evolution, consciousness and complexity, "a time of soul searching," as an article in the *Times Higher Education Supplement* called it.[54] This may help to bring the sciences and humanities more closely together, but science alone cannot provide us with the energy resources we need for dealing with the great issues facing the global community today: the issues of poverty, violence, environmental disaster and the survival and quality of human life. Spiritual resources are required to decide on the right values and actions, and take on the responsibility for the development of the earth and the human community. The deepest spiritual energy resources are found in the "various currents of faith . . . still active on earth," the religions of the world, which preserve and pass on to us the "fragments of vision" and "experiences of contact" with the supreme Spirit.[55] It is the spiritual resources preserved in the religions of the world that can best animate and maintain the human zest for life and provide us with the necessary energy for further development.

Teilhard envisaged a closer coming together of the different religions and their collaboration in working toward common aims beneficial for the whole human community. But it is always and everywhere the fire of love that he sees as the strongest source of empowerment for transformative action in the world. Christianity is for him more than anything else a religion of love. Teilhard describes Christian love as "a specifically new state of consciousness" and sees it as one of the most distinctive elements of Christianity:

> It is a phenomenon of capital importance for the science of man that, over an appreciable region of the earth, a zone of thought has appeared and grown in which a genuine universal love has not only been conceived and preached, but has also been shown to be psychologically possible and operative in practice. It is all the more capital inasmuch as, far from decreasing, the movement seems to wish to gain still greater speed and intensity.[56]

If we want to sustain and feed the zest for life and spur our efforts not simply to ensure the survival of the human species but to create a better life for all, it is necessary to have faith and ever more faith—faith in the sense of a spiritually empowering vision. This is not a faith that simply affirms and follows traditional rites and doctrines. It is a faith fired by the power of the Spirit; it is a faith that works and sensitizes our eyes, ears and soul to "recognize God's hand and voice in the world."[57] Only such a faith has access to the deepest wells of spiritual energy—and that makes all the difference to human life.

Teilhard's vision of spirit in evolution and of the transformative power of spirituality in human life can make an important contribution to contemporary debates about consciousness and spirituality, about the place of spiritual development in human growth and education. Teilhard once described his own position as standing "at a privileged crossroads in the world; . . . in my twofold character of priest and scientist, I have felt passing through me, in particularly exhilarating and varied conditions, the double stream of human and divine forces."[58] His life's work consisted in describing "the features of the resplendent image that has been disclosed to me in the universe," a vision that consisted in "approaching the vast disorder of things from a certain angle, suddenly to see their obscurity and discord become transformed in a vibration that passes all description, inexhaustible in the richness of its tones and its notes, interminable in the perfection of its unity."[59] It was a vision of the ultimate unity of things in God. It was a vision of faith.

As Teilhard wrote in *Le Milieu Divin,* we need such a faith to sustain us, we need to believe:

> If we do not believe, the waves engulf us, the winds blow, nourishment fails, sickness lays us low or kills us, the divine power is impotent or remote. If, on the other hand, we believe, the waters are welcoming and sweet, the bread is multiplied, our eyes are open, the dead rise again, the power of God is, as it were, drawn from Him by force and spreads throughout all nature . . .
>
> Under the influence of our faith, the universe is capable, without outwardly changing its characteristics, of becoming more supple, more fully animate—of being "sur-animated."
>
> If we believe, then everything is illuminated and takes shape around us: chance is seen to be order, success assumes an incorruptible plenitude, suffering becomes a visit and caress of God.[60]

CHAPTER FOUR

Christ in All Things

A Divine Center at the Heart of the Universe

ༀ

Many of Teilhard de Chardin's essays contain specific suggestions for further constructive theological work, particularly in christology. Seeing Christ in all things and all things in Christ touches the heart of Teilhard's vision. It is a perspective that unlocks all others and represents one of the most essential aspects of his thinking. However, as with all his ideas, his work here is much neglected by contemporary religious thinkers. It is almost tragic how the exile Teilhard endured during his life is perpetuated beyond his death. His thought continues to be ignored among the foremost Christian theologians of today, at least as far as Anglo-Saxon writers are concerned.

Teilhard's ideas are neither discussed by current writers on contemporary spirituality nor mentioned by theologians. A recent, up-to-date collection of theological texts for students[1] does not even refer to his work in its section on christology. Yet Teilhard makes a particularly important and original contribution to modern christological thought. As one commentator has rightly observed: "Although Teilhard created no finished theological system, his writings on Christology over almost forty years made, through their cumulative effect, the most impressive systematic contribution in modern times to the idea of a cosmic Christ."[2] But it is rare indeed that one finds references to his christological ideas. This proves once again that Teilhard's work is simply ignored rather than critically debated. It is almost as if a conspiracy of silence had descended to suppress his daring and courageous thought, which stands in a great and honorable tradition of doing theology while also providing much of the fuel needed for rekindling the light of Christian faith and strengthening the dynamic power of Christian spirituality.

The Heart of Teilhard's Faith

In the last chapter I quoted Teilhard's words on the power of faith, and the great need for ever greater faith today. For Teilhard faith had many aspects and consisted of many stages. Faith is not blind believing, but is linked to intelligence and knowledge. He meant by "faith" any "adherence of our intelligence to a general view of the universe . . . The essential note of the psychological act of faith is . . . to see as possible and to accept as more probable, a conclusion which, because it envelopes so much in space and time, goes far beyond all its analytical premises. *To believe is to achieve an intellectual synthesis* . . . All around us, every life is born from another life, or from a 'pre-life' . . . Similarly, I maintain, in the domain of beliefs, *every faith is born from a faith*. This form of birth . . . does not exclude reasoning . . . *To believe is to develop an act of synthesis whose first origin is inapprehensible.*"[3]

Teilhard de Chardin's own faith needed such an intellectual synthesis integrally linked to his scientific research and knowledge and to the features of the modern world as experienced today. It was a deeply religious faith centered on God, a God present in all things and experiences. Teilhard could not tolerate a dualistic attitude whereby the world we live in, whether the world of our ordinary experience or the immensity of the world around us, divides us from God.

To make people "see and make them feel"[4] the presence of God everywhere was Teilhard's primary aim. Although profoundly shaped by traditional, orthodox Christian piety, he was also a truly modern man. His critically enquiring mind probed the depths of personal subjectivity and tested the constructive powers of consciousness; it also experienced the terrifying force of unanswerable questions and doubt, and the uncertain search for one's own identity. Not unlike the thought experiments of other philosophers before him, Teilhard descended into his own depth to explore the frontiers of the mind and sense the frightening abyss opening up beneath him:

> I allowed my consciousness to sweep back to the farthest limit of my body, to ascertain whether I might not extend outside myself. I stepped down into the most hidden depths of my being, lamp in hand and ears alert, to discover whether, in the deepest recesses of the blackness within me, I might not see the glint of the waters of the current that flows on, whether I might not hear the murmur of their mysterious waters that rise from the uttermost depths and will burst forth no man knows where. With terror and intoxicating emotion, I realized that my own poor trifling existence was one with the immensity of all that is and all that is still in the process of becoming . . .
>
> Countless radiations run through me in every direction, and I am, in some way, no more than the place where they meet or conflict with one another . . .
>
> I am, obviously, free. But what does my freedom represent other than an imperceptible point buried in an indeterminate mass of laws and relationships that I cannot, by and large, control? . . .
>
> If we step down into ourselves, we shall be horrified to find there, *beneath the man of surface relationships and reflection,* an unknown—a man as yet hardly emerged from unconsciousness, still . . . no more than half-awake."[5]

Teilhard wanted to shake people into wakefulness, into greater awareness so that they can experience "the countenance of the world"[6] within them and recognize in the features of the great cosmos the lineaments of God. The contemporary crisis of faith, of certainty, is for him part of an immense process toward a *new awakening* in people's minds and hearts, which he prophetically predicted. He thought that

> to come up to his full measure, *he* [the human being] *must become conscious of his infinite capacity for carrying himself still further;* he must realize the duties it

involves, and he must feel its intoxicating wonder. He must abandon all the illusions of narrow individuals and extend himself, intellectually and emotionally, to the dimensions of the universe: and this even though, his mind reeling at the prospect of his new greatness, he should think that he is already in possession of the divine, is God himself, or is himself the artisan of Godhead.[7]

These are extraordinary words, especially when linked to our present knowledge about the dimensions of the universe, but also when set within their own context of writing. This view was expressed during Easter week of 1916 amid the trench warfare near Dunkirk. Given this setting, one cannot understand this declaration except, as he himself did, as an "impassioned profession of . . . faith in the richness and value of the world,"[8] but a world energized and activated, created, sustained, propelled forward and upward by the vast, unfathomable powers and presence of the Spirit. Much later, a few years before the end of his life, he reaffirmed this faith in "the diaphany of the Divine at the heart of the universe on fire" and of "Christ. His Heart. A Fire," capable of penetrating everywhere and, gradually, spreading everywhere.[9]

Like his famous countryman Blaise Pascal, Teilhard emphasized the greater role of the heart over reason, of love and feeling, in our knowledge of God. This is due to a deeply experiential, mystical encounter with God rather than to abstract theological reasoning, which could not have produced the vision of fire that compelled him. When Pascal died in 1662, a note was found in his garment that movingly describes his powerful spiritual experience, expressed in the words:

FIRE
God of Abraham, God of Isaac, God of
Jacob, not of the
philosophers and scholars.
Certitude, certitude, feeling, joy, peace.
God of Jesus Christ.
. . . .
Thy God will be my God
. . . .

This is the eternal life, that they know thee
as the only true
God, and the one whom thou hast sent,
Jesus Christ.

Teilhard left a similar document when he died, not sewn into his clothes but standing on his desk. It was a picture of the radiant *heart of Christ*, personally inscribed with "My Litany" on the front and back of the picture. It speaks vividly about God, about Christ and Christianity, about Jesus and his heart. I would like to quote a few passages from this litany:

The God of evolution
The Christic, the Trans-Christ
Sacred Heart . . . the motor of evolution
the heart of evolution
the heart of matter
The heart of God . . . the world-zest
The activant of Christianity . . . the essence
of all energy
. . . .
Heart of the world's heart
Focus of ultimate and universal energy
Centre of the cosmic sphere of cosmogenesis
Heart of Jesus, heart of evolution, unite me
to yourself.[10]

This litany sums up Teilhard's faith of a lifetime, the fervent belief that the world has a heart, a center. The immense cosmic process of becoming has a focus, a pole, and the divine fire of God's heart and love provides all the zest and energy the world needs. The essence of this energy is activated and can be tapped into through Christianity, through the fire and power of the Christian faith, whose potential for love, for "amorizing" the world, must be raised to incandescence.[11] Teilhard sees Christianity as the religion of evolution par excellence, and its God as the "God of evolution." In 1953, two years before his death, he wrote a brief note on this "God of Evolution" on the feast of Christ the King.[12] In it he first states that unfortunately Christianity seems often closely

connected with people who belong to rather backward-look-
ing and undeveloped groups in the contemporary world.
Among the rank and file of the faithful, and even in religious
orders, "Christianity still to some degree provides a *shelter*
for the 'modern soul,' but it no longer *clothes* it, nor *satisfies*
it, nor *leads* it. Something has gone wrong—and so something, in the area of faith and religion, must be supplied without delay on this planet. The question is, what is it we are
looking for?"[13]

Teilhard was looking for a God of evolution, a God whose
image is truly commensurate with the complex dimensions
of our universe; a God who is not an outsider, a prime mover,
but is deeply involved with the entire cosmic process of which
we form an integral part; a truly living God, with us here and
now, fully incarnate in matter and all-becoming. For him, the
essence of Christianity is a belief in the unification of the
world in God through the incarnation. It is because of this
central belief that Teilhard saw Christianity—not western
Christianity as we know it but a much more inclusive and
all-embracing Christianity—as a "religion of action,"[14] a religion of evolution, and a religion of the future.

Evolution is an ongoing event, and the coming of Christ is
also a continuing process and event, a *"Christic advent,"* which
has not yet come to a stop nor found its true fulfillment. As
he wrote in 1953:

> in a universe in which we can no longer seriously enter-
> tain the idea that thought is an exclusively terrestrial
> phenomenon, Christ must no longer be *constitutionally*
> restricted in his operation to a mere "redemption" of our
> planet . . .
>
> In the eyes of everyone who is alive to the reality of the
> cosmic movement of complexity-consciousness which
> produces us, Christ, as still presented to the world of
> classical theology, is both too confined (localized) astro-
> nomically, and evolutively too extrinsic, to be able to
> "cephalise" the universe as we now see it.[15]

Who then is Christ for Teilhard? What is the Christ event?
Let us explore Teilhard's understanding of Christ and his

emphasis on the central importance of Christ for Christianity today.

Discovering the Features of Teilhard's Christ

Most specific to Teilhard's understanding is the notion of the *cosmic Christ*. This is so important and central that he could argue that the cosmic is a third nature of Christ, along with his human and divine nature. We know of numerous contemporary arguments against a fully incarnational christology, described as the "myth" and "metaphor" of "God Incarnate."[16] One must ask how such arguments attack an incarnational doctrine, which is understood much too literally, but also how far contemporary theological debates are still wedded to categories of classical theology and theism that remain too fixed and static, too constricted and constrained, because they are based on an essentialist and substantive ontotheology that no longer works today.

If there is an urgent need for a sympathetic restatement of incarnational theology, Teilhard's ideas may well provide some inspiration for such a development. Today more than ever before we are aware of the many Christs of Christianity, the many faces of Jesus expressed in different ages and cultures. By comparison, classical Chalcedonian christology is rather exclusive and monolithic, not leaving room for the pluralistic christologies we need in order to account for the different Christs experienced by faith—not only the Christ of dogma, but the Christ of piety and devotion, the Christ of ascetics and mystics, the Christ of political and social radicalism, the Christ of peace and justice, the Christ of love and forgiveness, the Christ of healing and reconciliation, the Christ of transformation and renewal.

Teilhard did not explicitly enquire into the significance of Christ for different cultures, but he understood the incarnation as a universal, ongoing process that must always be linked to the specificity of context and experience. God's word to humanity is not primarily the word spoken in a book, in sacred literature, but it is a word that is incarnate, not only as a *human* being, but present as *an element* in *all beings*, in all created reality, all of which needs completion, fulfillment and redemption. God is incarnate in matter, in flesh, in all of creation, in the cosmos. The incarnation of Christ becomes extended to the dimensions of the cosmos; it is an event and mystery of cosmic extension. As he wrote in *The Mass on the World*: "Through your own incarnation, my God, all matter is henceforth incarnate."[17] God is "incarnate in the world." We are all together "carried in the one world-womb; yet each of us is our own little microcosm in which the Incarnation is wrought independently with degrees of intensity, and shades that are incommunicable." Teilhard firmly believed that everything around him "is the body and blood of the Word."[18]

Thus Teilhard's spirituality is characterized by going to God via the universe in its process of development and becoming. The evolutionary process is both cosmic and christic in the sense that creation since its beginning is developing toward its complete fullness in what Teilhard calls *"Christ-Omega."* This concept has a twofold foundation: It is the outcome of combining his vision of faith, grounded in Bible and tradition, with the evolutionary perspectives of modern science.

Teilhard's biblical references are mostly to the cosmic hymns of St. Paul and to the gospel of St. John. His school education had included a sound training in Greek; later, as a theology student in Hastings, during the years 1908-1912, he also learned Hebrew. His theological training included studying the New Testament in Greek, which led him to make detailed summaries of all the passages speaking of Christ and creation—passages in which he found his own experience of the ultimate unity and oneness of all of creation confirmed. The cosmic hymns of St. Paul, especially in Colossians, resonated strongly in him. Here he felt that the incarnation event was linked to the density of life stretching out from its fossil forms in the distant past through present life and nature toward some future point of maturation. Was all creation not like a continuous stream of living matter, energy and spirit, a cosmic web animated by divine life itself? It was the occasion for an incarnate presence that took on everywhere the figure and face of Jesus Christ as "the soul of the world."

Teilhard's mystical devotion to Christ responded also very

vividly to the *humanity of Jesus*. It is a devotion of great personal intimacy and lyrical beauty. This is particularly well expressed in the early writings, which include his own prayers and often repeat the name of Jesus. In Chapter 2, I quoted a passage from the three stories "Christ in the World of Matter" (1916), which movingly describes Christ's face and eyes. In the important essay "The Mystical Milieu" (1917), Teilhard outlined the progress of the mystic through traversing a successive set of circles. This description reflects his own outer and inner journey. He called this essay simply *"an introduction to mysticism,"*[19] not a description of its most sublime states. It is a journey through a universe on fire with the presence of the Spirit, culminating in God's omnipresence, centered and gathered up into *one single point*: the person of Jesus:

> His power animated all energy. His mastering life ate into every other life, to assimilate it to himself . . . Since first, Lord, you said, *'Hoc est corpus meum,'* not only the bread on the altar, but (to some degree) everything in the universe that nourishes the soul for the life of Spirit and Grace, has become *yours* and has become *divine*—it is divinized, divinizing, and divinizable. Every presence makes me feel that you are near me; every touch is the touch of your hand; every necessity transmits to me a pulsation of your will. And so true is this, that everything around me . . . has become for me . . . in some way, the substance of your heart:
> Jesus!
> That is why it is impossible for me, Lord . . . to look on your face without seeing in it the *radiance* of every reality and goodness. In the mystery of your mystical body—your cosmic body—you sought to feel the echo of every joy and every fear that moves each single one of all the countless cells that make up mankind . . .
> When I think of you, Lord, I cannot say whether it is in this place that I find you more, or in that place . . . whether I am contemplating you or whether I am suffering—whether I rue my faults or find union—whether it is you I love or the whole sum of others. Every affection,

every desire, every possession, every light, every depth,
every harmony, and every ardour glitters with equal
brilliance . . . in the inexpressible *Relationship* that is
being set up between me and you: Jesus![20]

This is again a very vivid passage wherein Teilhard evokes
Jesus' concrete presence by appealing to the touch of his hand,
the radiance of his face, the mystery of his body. Jesus is a
person of "superabundant unity," of divine fullness which
Teilhard describes as "the Ocean of Life, the life that penetrates and quickens us," a person whose mystical body is a
"cosmic body."[21]

Teilhard loved the Greek Fathers and knew their works
well. He was familiar with their teaching on incarnation and
divinization, especially on the possible deification—the
theosis—of the human being. For Teilhard creation, incarnation and redemption do not happen as a single event, completed once and for all; he sees them as ongoing processes
that culminate in "pleromization," in a fulfillment and plenitude where all is made whole and one. As he wrote:

Creation, Incarnation, Redemption. Until today, these
three fundamental mysteries of the Christian faith,
while indissolubly linked *in fact* in the history of the
world, have remained *logically* independent of one another . . . If these three mysteries are transposed from
the old cosmos (static, limited, and open at every moment to rearrangement) into the modern universe (or-
ganically welded by its space-time into a single evolutive
whole), they tend to form but one mystery . . . to create
is for God to unite himself to his work, that is to say in one
way or another to involve himself in the world by incarnation. And is not "to be incarnate" *ipso facto* to share in
the sufferings and evils inherent in the painfully concen-
trating multiple? Creation, Incarnation, Redemption:
seen in this light, the three mysteries become in reality
no more . . . than the aspects of one and the same
fundamental process: they are aspects of a *fourth* mystery . . . it is the mystery of the creative union of the
world in God, or Pleromization.[22]

He linked this "pleromization" to a "trinitization,"[23] for his vision, though so much centered on Christ, is truly trinitarian: The entire cosmic process is seen as going to the Father through the Son in the Spirit.

It is in *The Mass on the World* that we find some of his strongest and most personal statements about Jesus Christ, Lord of the universe, center of universal consecration and communion. In this work, written in 1923 somewhere near the Yellow River in China when there was no opportunity to say mass, Teilhard expressed with great poetic power the symbolic offering-up of the whole world to God. This text provides undeniable evidence that for him Christ is inclusive not only of all of humanity, but of all of creation, all of life, all beings and elements in the cosmos. Christ is not exhausted by the human Jesus, but means ever so much more. He is the fullness that embraces also the immense richness of creation.

As Teilhard admits in *The Mass on the World:* "As long as I could see—or dared see—in you, Lord Jesus, only the man who lived two thousand years ago, the sublime moral teacher, the Friend, the Brother, my love remained timid and constrained. Friends, brothers, wise men: have we not many of these around us, great souls, chosen souls, and much closer to us?" It is above all the power of the resurrection that makes Christ "shine forth from within all the forces of the earth," makes him into the "Sovereign" of the cosmos to whom Teilhard can surrender himself. This central position of Christ in the cosmos is symbolically expressed in the image of the heart, "a furnace of fire," around which the contours of the body melt away and become enlarged beyond all measure until the only features he can distinguish "are those of the face of a world which has burst into flame."[24]

Teilhard then moves into a prayer of great power and beauty that includes another anthropomorphic description of the figure of Christ:

> Glorious Lord Christ: the divine influence secretly diffused and active in the depths of matter, and the dazzling centre where all the innumerable fibres of the manifold meet; power as implacable as the world and as warm as life; you whose forehead is of the whiteness of snow, whose eyes are of fire, and whose feet are brighter than

molten gold; you whose hands imprison the stars; you
who are the first and the last, the living and the dead and
the risen again; you who gather into your exuberant
unity every beauty, every affinity, every energy, every
mode of existence; it is you to whom my being cried out
with a desire as vast as the universe, "In truth you are my
Lord and my God."[25]

This is a powerful proclamation of faith and surrender, but it
is also a vision of a cosmic person, of what the Indian Vedas
call *purusha*. Anne Hunt Overzee, in her study *The Body Divine*,[26] has shown how Teilhard's vision of the divine form as
Lord of the cosmos has an extraordinary parallel in the vivid
description the eleventh-century Hindu theologian Ramanuja
has given of the cosmic vision of Vishnu, his incomparable
beauty and splendor, in the *Bhagavad Gita*. Both theologians—the Hindu Ramanuja in the eleventh century and the
Christian Teilhard de Chardin in the twentieth—see the
Lord's unique and proper form as pervading, encompassing
and illuminating the world, which is his body. The world as
God's body is a rich metaphor for contemporary ecological
and sacramental theology, and much insight and material,
unexplored so far, can be drawn from both theologians.

It was Teilhard's particular concern to express again and
again God's universal influence and omnipresence, uphold-
ing everything in existence in and through Christ: "Nothing,
Lord Jesus, can subsist outside your flesh . . . All of us, ines-
capably, exist in you the universal *milieu* in which and through
which all things live and have their being."[27] If others are
called to proclaim the splendors of God as pure Spirit, Teilhard
thought his own particular vocation was to preach "the innu-
merable prolongations of your incarnate Being in the world
of matter . . . the mystery of your flesh, you the Soul shining
forth through all that surrounds us."[28]

The sacramental offering of "the mass" on the whole world
finishes with the words:

It is to your body in this its fullest extention—that is, to
the world become through your power and my faith the
glorious living crucible in which everything melts away
in order to be born anew; it is to this that I dedicate

myself . . . with the all too feeble resources of my scientific knowledge, with my religious vows, with my priesthood, and (most dear to me) with my deepest human convictions. It is in this dedication, Lord Jesus, I desire to live, in this I desire to die.[29]

Such a vision invites the Christian to develop "an ever-increasing awareness" of God's omnipresence, which leads to "a blessed desire to go on advancing, discovering, fashioning and experiencing the world so as to penetrate ever further and further" into Christ and through Christ into God.[30] Seeing Christ in all things and all things in Christ is what Teilhard, following Blondel, called "pan-Christism,"[31] but what is perhaps more appropriately characterized as "panchristic mysticism." It is a magnificent transposition of the Ignatian theme of seeing God in all things and all things in God.

In his annual retreats, Teilhard regularly followed *The Spiritual Exercises* of St. Ignatius, as Jesuits are wont to do. This key text and spiritual classic, written by the founder of the Jesuits in the early sixteenth century, encapsulates Ignatius's "dynamic spirituality which was ordered toward both personal spiritual growth and energetic apostolic endeavour,"[32] but Teilhard transposed its message from a fixed, static world into a world of evolution, caught in the universal flux of becoming. The "diaphany" of God in and through all things is connected for him with the adoration and proclamation of "the ever greater Christ" involved in the evolutionary development toward greater plenitude, a process he also called "Christogenesis." This is certainly a high christology that enhances and expands traditional christological thinking by adding new categories, especially when Teilhard speaks of the universal, cosmic Christ, and of Christ-Omega.

The Fullness of the Universal Christ

We find a rich theology of the body of Christ in Teilhard's work, which deserves further detailed study. I can mention only a few aspects here. The body of Christ has several different meanings in Teilhard's writings. It can refer to the person of Jesus of Nazareth, but it is also a body that forms a personal center for humanity and the material world. It is a physical, organic center, a christic element in all things, so that all things can be an opening, an occasion for a disclosure of Christ to us. A detailed analysis of Teilhard's understanding of Christ was undertaken by Christopher Mooney in 1966 in his *Teilhard de Chardin and the Mystery of Christ*.[33] Mooney assessed Teilhard's thought as a possible catalyst toward further developments in christology, but this has not happened yet.[34]

Some sixteen years later, in 1982, James A. Lyons published a comparative study, *The Cosmic Christ in Origen and Teilhard de Chardin*.[35] This provides particularly helpful elements for further christological reflection by tracing cosmic Christ terminology from patristic times to the modern era. Both Origen's and Teilhard's visions of the cosmic Christ are based on the New Testament, but Origen gave the theme a Platonizing treatment whereas Teilhard dealt with it in an evolutionary manner, allowing for new christological developments, which theologians have not yet acknowledged. However, such a development is urgently needed in the light of modern science, especially given the contemporary knowledge of cosmology and evolutionary biology. Lyons concluded that the rise of cosmic Christ language has introduced a newly perceived issue into christological discussion, which he saw as a legitimate, necessary and ongoing issue: "It is legitimate not only because it is founded on scriptural data and continues matters that were raised in theological traditions of the past; it is also at the point where contemporary views about the universe make an impact on the Christian faith. It is a necessary issue, since it upholds the Christian belief, that however vast and strange the universe may turn out to be, it is Christ who is at the centre of all. It is an ongoing issue because the teaching Church has scarcely begun to concern itself with the cosmic Christ."[36]

Teilhard had expressed this vision of Christ as the center of all development and growth in his first essay of 1916, where he wrote:

Since Jesus was born, and grew to his full stature, and died, everything has continued to move forward *because Christ is not yet fully formed*: he has not yet gathered about him the last folds of his robe of flesh and of love which is made up of his faithful followers. The mystical Christ has not yet attained to his full growth; and therefore the same is true of the cosmic Christ. Both of these are simultaneously in the state of being and of becoming; and it is from the prolongation of this process of becoming that all created activity ultimately springs. Christ is the end-point of the evolution, even the *natural* evolution, of all beings, and therefore evolution is holy.[37]

This passage shows clearly how the human Jesus grows into the cosmic and mystical Christ, and how all beings, all evolutionary becoming, are incorporated into him. As I mentioned earlier, Teilhard was not primarily interested in the human Jesus, the historical person born in Palestine about two thousand years ago. As he wrote to one of his friends in 1926:

I do not like that evangelism which limits itself to a glorification of the purely human or moral qualities of Jesus. If Jesus were no more than "a father, a mother, a brother, a sister" to us, I would have no need of Him; and, in a sense, the past does not interest me. What I "ask" of Christ is that He be a Force that is immense, present, universal, as real (more real) than Matter, which I can *adore*; in short, I ask Him to be for me the Universe: complete, concentrated, and capable of being adored. This is why, while acknowledging the irreplaceable value of the first three Gospels in presenting the real, historical *beginnings* of Christ . . . I prefer Saint John and Saint Paul, who really present in the *resurrected* Christ a being as vast as the World of all time. Have you read, for example, the beginning of the Epistle to the Colossians (Chapter I, verses 12-23), and tried to give it the full, organic meaning it requires? Here Christ appears as a true soul of the World. It is only thus that I love Him."[38]

He wrote this from China in a letter to Ida Treat, dated October 30, 1926. Already in 1918 he had entitled one of his essays "The Soul of the World,"[39] where he spoke of this soul as a distinct reality, understood as an immanent center and focus of energy for the world. Teilhard felt that such a soul might be vivid and concrete even for those who do not believe in Christ, although for him such a soul is linked to "a cosmic element divinized by Christ."[40] From 1920 onward he referred to the "universal Christ,"[41] which he understands as "the organic center of the entire universe," a center "not only of moral and religious effort, but of all physical and spiritual growth."[42] He criticizes theologians for not recognizing *the primacy of the organic over the juridical*"[43] and for interpreting the "mystical body" in an analogous rather than a realist sense. He refers to a long series of Johannine and Pauline texts in the New Testament in which "the physical supremacy of Christ over the universe is so magnificently expressed," so much so that only "timid minds . . . escape the awesome realism of these repeated statements."[44] Paul's "theandric Christ" becomes for Teilhard the cosmic Christ, the supreme center of spiritual consistence of the entire universe, present as a universal, incarnate element throughout the world: "The presence of the Incarnate Word penetrates everything, as a universal element. It shines at the common heart of things, as a center that is infinitely intimate to them and at the same time . . . infinitely distant."[45] In later years he calls this element the "Super-Christ," by which he means *not another* Christ[46] but a term "to express that excess of greatness assumed in our consciousness by the Person of Christ in step with the awakening of our minds to the super-dimensions of the world and of mankind."[47]

This is "Christ the Evolver"—not Christ the King and Master, whose universal power over creation is primarily seen in an extrinsic and juridical manner, but a Christ who "physically and literally . . . *fills all things*: at no instant in the world, is there any element of the world that has moved, that moves, that ever shall move, outside the directing flood he pours into them." It is Christ who consummates the world and effects its final plenitude. All structual lines of the world converge upon him, and "it is he who *gives its consistence* to the entire edifice of matter and Spirit."[48] Thus for Teilhard, "the light of Christ, far from being eclipsed by the growing brilliance of the ideas of the future, of scientific research and of progress, is coming into prominence as the very central core destined to sustain their ardour."[49]

The universal Christ is for Teilhard "a synthesis of Christ and the universe," not a new godhead,[50] but an inevitable development of the mystery of the incarnation reinterpreted in the light of modern science. He writes:

> If we Christians wish to *retain* in Christ the very quali-
> ties on which his power and our worship are based, we
> have no better way—no other way, even—of doing so
> than fully to accept the most modern concepts of evolu-
> tion. Under the combined pressure of science and phi-
> losophy, we are being forced, experientially and intellec-
> tually, to accept the world as a coordinated system of
> activity which is gradually rising up towards freedom
> and consciousness. The only satisfactory way of inter-
> preting this process . . . is to regard it as irreversible and
> convergent. Thus, ahead of us, a *universal cosmic center*
> is taking on definition, in which everything reaches its
> term, in which everything is explained, is felt, and is
> ordered. It is, then, in this physical pole of universal
> evolution that we must, in my view, locate and recognize
> the plenitude of Christ. For *in no other type of cosmos,*
> and *in no other place* can any being, *no matter how divine
> he be,* carry out the function of universal consolidation
> and universal animation which Christian dogma at-
> tributes to Christ. By disclosing a world-peak, evolution
> makes Christ possible, just as Christ, by giving meaning
> and direction to the world, makes evolution possible.[51]

The full recognition and acceptance of the universal Christ requires a new theological orientation and reinterpretation of Christianity, or what Teilhard sometimes calls a "neo-Chris-tianity." But a Christ renewed by contact with the modern world is still the same Christ as the Christ of the gospel; it is in fact an *even greater Christ*. Teilhard could say about his position: "I have been reproached as being an innovator. In truth, the more I have thought about the magnificent cosmic attributes lavished by St. Paul on the risen Christ, and the more I have considered the masterful significance of the Chris-tian virtues, the more clearly have I realized that Christianity takes on its full value only when extended . . . to its cosmic dimensions."[52]

Christology and the Renewal of Christianity

Teilhard saw himself as an "apostle of the cosmic Christ" and was convinced that if a greater place were accorded to the universal, cosmic Christ, this would lead to a "new era for Christianity," an era of "interior liberation and expansion."[53] He was a stringent critic of his own church, which he sometimes saw as no longer truly catholic, truly universal, but as "defending a system, a sect."[54] One of his harshest judgments on the Church dates from 1929, perhaps the harshest ever, according to Henri de Lubac:

> . . . the only thing that I can be: a voice that repeats, *opportune et importune,* that the Church will waste away so long as she does not escape from the factitious world of verbal theology, of quantitative sacramentalism, and over-refined devotions in which she is enveloped, so as to reincarnate herself in the real aspirations of mankind . . . Of course I can see well enough what is paradoxical in this attitude: if I need Christ and the Church I should accept Christ as he is presented by the Church, with its burden of rites, administration and theology . . . But now I can't get away from the evidence that the moment has come when the Christian impulse should "save Christ" from the hands of the clerics so that the world may be saved.[55]

Here he is attacking those who retreat into the past, theological writers "whose 'dead prose' is never brought to life by any 'religious sap' and in whom only 'truths already digested a hundred times and with no living essence' are to be found."[56] Yet for Teilhard Christian faith and spirituality can be revitalized and draw new energies from an enlarged understanding of Christ:

> By making plain the splendors of the universal Christ, Christianity, without ceasing to be for the earth the

water that purifies and the oil that soothes, acquires a new value. By the very fact that it provides the earth's aspirations with a goal that is at once *immense, concrete* and *assured,* it rescues the earth from disorder, the uncertainties, and the nausea that are the most terrible of tomorrow's dangers. It provides the fire that inspires man's effort. In other words, it is seen to be the form of faith that is most fitted to modern needs: a religion for progress—the very religion of progress of the earth—I would go so far as to say the very religion of evolution.[57]

Teilhard made repeated suggestions for a renewal of Christian theology,[58] a renewal of Christian life and holiness, a renewal of Christian spirituality and mysticism.[59] In fact, it was particularly toward the end of his life that he was most concerned with these themes of renewal. Returning from China to Europe after the end of the Second World War, he noticed especially the growing credibility gap between traditional Christianity and the modern world. Had he not written years before that "we must, *with all that is human in us,* re-think our religion . . . *Christianity must at last accept unreservedly the new dimensions (spatial, temporal and psychological) of the world around us."*[60] As a Christian he did not believe that Christianity would disappear, but he recognized that it was undergoing a period of profound transition and "that Christianity (exactly like the mankind it embraces) is reaching the end of one of the natural cycles of its existence."[61]

Theologically he considered it important to complete the unfinished task of the christological developments of the first five Christian centuries by reflecting on the cosmic nature of Christ. He called for a new "Nicea," not to deal once more with Christ and the Trinity but to deal with the problem of a newly understood relationship between Christ and the universe. Three Christs have to be recognized and exalted: a historical, a cosmic and a transcendent Christ. Ewert Cousins, in *Christ of the 21st Century,*[62] considers Teilhard's vision of the cosmic Christ an important part of "the fullness of the mystery of Christ," which we have to rediscover for a renewal of Christian spirituality. It is as Teilhard wrote: "Christianity is much more than a fixed system, presented to us once and for all, of truths which have to be accepted and preserved literally. For all its resting on a core of 'revelation,' it represents in fact a spiritual attitude which is continually developing; it is the development of a Christic consciousness in step with, and to meet the needs of, the growing consciousness of humankind."[63] Such growing consciousness was for Teilhard closely connected with a fuller, richer development of spirituality.

Can we see signs of such a development in our present world? We are experiencing so much strife, dissension, poverty, violence, injustice and doubt that it seems difficult to observe spiritual growth and development. Yet there are many signs of a renewed interest in spirituality, a growth in the publication of "spiritual classics," in the retreat and meditation movement. Our sensate and materialistic culture leaves many people deeply dissatified. They yearn for a richer, fuller vision and way of being human. Teilhard was of the view that many of the neohumanisms of the twentieth century dehumanize us whereas the still living forms of theisms, including Christianity, tend not to develop our humanity to the full because they "are still systematically closed to the wide horizons and great winds of Cosmogenesis, and can no longer truly be said to feel with the Earth—an Earth whose internal frictions they can still lubricate like a soothing oil, but whose driving energies they cannot animate as they should."[64]

Teilhard's large, complex oeuvre contains many seminal ideas for theology, always presented as *suggestions, explorations* and *evocative reflections,* rather than as a systematically developed body of thought. His primary concern and commitment were deeply pastoral, missionary and apologetic in the largest sense. But can his ideas speak to Christians today? Or can they make sense to people of other faiths? Is his universal Christ perhaps too exclusive, too dominant to leave room for otherness? These are some of the questions to be explored in the following chapters.

One can approach Teilhard on many different levels. He was a faithful member of the Catholic church and the Jesuit order; he was a powerful witness of the Christian gospel; he wrestled with the question of God in contemporary culture; he perceived the urgent need for a greater coherence between science, religion and mysticism. But his person stands above all for the spiritually transforming power and dynamic of the Christian faith, for a vision centered on the heart and essence of Christianity: the belief in God incarnate—incarnate in humanity and the world, in cosmos and matter.

Teilhard adhered to this faith with immense saintliness and suffering. It was not an easily won faith, but one of great effort, cost and struggle. Teilhard's spirituality was not only one of union and divine adoration, but quite literally also a spirituality of resistance and strength grown out of affliction. His was a truly christic consciousness, a mystical spirituality of a fresh and original kind, about which I shall speak in the next chapter. But before I do so, I would like to quote from Teilhard's "Prayer to the Ever-Greater Christ":

> Because, Lord, by every innate impulse and through all the hazards of my life I have been driven ceaselessly to search for you and to set you in the heart of the universe of matter, I shall have the joy, when death comes, of closing my eyes amidst the splendour of a universal transparency aglow with fire . . .
>
> Lord of consistence and union, you whose *distinguishing mark* and *essence* is the power indefinitely to grow greater, without distortion or loss of continuity, to the measure of the mysterious Matter whose Heart you fill and all whose movements you ultimately control—Lord of my childhood and Lord of my last days—God, complete in relation to yourself and yet, for us, continually being born . . .
>
> Let your universal Presence spring forth in a blaze that is at once Diaphany and Fire.
>
> O ever-greater Christ![65]

CHAPTER FIVE

Mysticism-in-Action

*An Empowering Vision of Christian Faith
and Love*

ᘒᘈᘒ

The previous chapter dealt with Teilhard de Chardin's
panchristic mysticism, his understanding of Christ as a
"christic element" present in all things, culminating in his
vision of Christ-Omega. His deeply mystical faith made him
perceive a "dazzling center" of matter, a divine center or heart
present in the immensely complex development of the universe. Although Teilhard studied the external world as a scientist, he could not fully make sense of all its features except
by combining the perspectives of both science and religion in
an all-embracing, new kind of mysticism.

This vision of faith was based on a fundamental trust in
life, and a deep faith in God. In spite of all the critical advances of modern science, Teilhard firmly upheld the reason-
ableness of such faith. In spite of the radical ambiguity of our
experiences, such faith can not only be seen to be reasonable,
but it is also a strongly empowering, energizing and transformative force in human life and society.

We are now living in a world where ever increasing knowledge presents us with immensely greater choices, but also
with ever greater uncertainties. Teilhard asked: What is the
effect of scientific advances on the development of thought?
What is the power of thought, of self-reflexivity, of social re-
flexivity on all of humankind together? Doors have been
opened to new horizons but "thought has never yet been stud-

ied in the same way as the immensities of matter, as a reality of cosmic and evolutionary nature. Let us take this step. Let us . . . analyse the properties and determine the place of the human phenomenon in the general history of the world."[1]

If we do this by examining not only the past, but also the direction of the future, we can appreciate Teilhard's questions of what we should do to help humanity advance: "What organizations shall we choose? What relations shall we form between peoples? What roads shall we open up? What morality adopt? Towards what ideal collect our energies? By what hope preserve in the heart of the human mass the sacred appetite for research and progress?" For Teilhard such questions were a call for reflection, and for responsible action to take up our task "to sublimate and save the spirit of the earth and of life. Not only to recognize evolution, but to make it continue in ourselves."[2]

The complex developments of modern science greatly challenge traditional religious thought. But Teilhard took this to be a creative, not a destructive challenge, a great opportunity for the deepening and strengthening of faith, not for its weakening and dilution. He called for "a new theological orientation"[3] but also for a new "mystical orientation" by bringing science and mysticism more closely together. He understood both science and religion as moving toward a goal, an "Omega," and he interpreted their movements as ultimately convergent. Thus he could speak of "a most revealing correspondence between the shapes . . . of the two confronting Omegas: that postulated by modern science, and that experienced by Christian mysticism."[4] To weld together science and mysticism might bring about "a great tide of released evolutive power."[5]

But what did Teilhard understand by the "phenomenon of mysticism" he so often mentions? How does mysticism relate to science? And what is this new mysticism of action so essential for a new world?

The Phenomenon of Mysticism

Teilhard's mysticism was one of union and communion, of adoration and celebration. His deepest desire was to adore

the Divine in all its expressions, forms and faces: "To adore
. . . That means to lose oneself in the unfathomable, to plunge
into the inexhaustible, to find peace in the incorruptible, to
be absorbed in defined immensity, to offer oneself to the fire
. . . and to give of one's deepest to that whose depth has no
end. Whom, then, can we adore?"[6]

Teilhard did not write about Christian mysticism merely
as an insider, as a Christian whose words were only addressed
to other Christians. On the contrary, his worldwide travels,
his numerous contacts with scientists from different cultural
and religious backgrounds, his meetings and friendships with
so many people, whether religious believers of different faiths,
atheists or militant communists, made him aware of the need
for translating the message of the gospel into a new idiom.

From his early days he was aware of his own pantheistic
inclinations and of his search for absolute unity. He often
spoke of his sense of a "feeling of the Whole" and referred to
the experience of "cosmic consciousness in our soul."[7] He described this experience as often "more diffuse than our personal consciousness, more intermittent, but perfectly well-
defined" and present in many ordinary people:

> a sort of feeling of the presence of all beings at the same
> time, so that they are not perceived as multiple and
> separate but as forming part of one and the same unit . . .
> Whether this consciousness of the universal is a reality,
> or whether it is the materialization of a wish, of an
> expectation—that is a question for the psychologists to
> answer, if they can. The least one may say is that many
> people have believed that they have experienced "cosmic
> consciousness" . . . at least it shows . . . how immensely
> strong is our feeling of the importance of the Whole.[8]

All Teilhard's early essays in the book *Writings in Time of
War* are shot through with reflections on cosmic consciousness, pantheism and mysticism. His mother had been the first
to introduce him to the Christian mystics, but he read widely
on mysticism throughout his life, not only texts by the Christian mystics but also studies on mystics from other traditions.
He was helped in this by his Jesuit confrère, Fr. Joseph

Maréchal, whom he first met in 1910. This priest-scholar, eminent philosopher and writer on mysticism, became an inspiring figure for him, whom he consulted more than once. Here was a Jesuit with a similar interest in science and religion who, moreover, published *Studies in the Psychology of the Mystics.*[9] One of these, "On the Feeling of Presence in Mystics and Non-Mystics," first appeared in 1908-1910 and discussed among others Hindu, Buddhist and Sufi mystics, but we do not know whether Teilhard read the article at that time.

However, it may well have been through meeting Maréchal that Teilhard first came across R. M. Bucke's much cited studies on cosmic consciousness and William James's *Varieties of Religious Experience,* both referred to in Maréchal's article. Teilhard always appreciated William James, whose *Varieties of Religious Experience* and *Pragmatism* he read during the later years of the First World War, together with popular French publications on comparative mysticism. He especially immersed himself in the Rhenish mystics, Tauler and Eckhardt, and he also consulted his former teacher, Fr. Henri Bremond, about the Christian mystics. No doubt Teilhard became aware of Bremond's famous work *Histoire littéraire du sentiment religieux,* published in 1916, which presented many hitherto unknown mystics to its readers.

Yet Teilhard was neither a systematic student of the mystics nor an expert on mystical literature. His essays often mention the names of individual mystics and include numerous remarks on the phenomenon of mysticism. He continued to have a strong interest in this until the end of his life. For example his notes of 1945, preserved in his *carnets de lecture,* contain several extracts from Maréchal's work and some intriguing comments on the different forms of Vedanta.[10] When he lived in Paris after the Second World War, he was able to meet practicing Hindus and Sufis whom he could ask about mystics in Hinduism and Islam, and he then also had an opportunity to undertake more systematic reading on mysticism. Whatever the importance of these contacts and notes for interpreting Teilhard's own particular synthesis and originality, his interest in mysticism was primarily a personal, experiential one, linked to his mystical temperament and world view.

Teilhard described himself more than once as a "pantheist by nature." The English scholar on mysticism, R. C. Zaehner, has said that throughout the First World War Teilhard "seems to have lived in an almost permanent state of 'cosmic consciousness.' "[11] Teilhard understood this consciousness as a feeling of expansion and fusion when in contact with the natural world, the earth. It is a deep inner experience wherein one allows oneself "to be rocked like a child by the great mother" in whose arms one has just woken.[12]

But such "communion with the earth" was not enough for him; it symbolized a state of fusion, without distinction or qualification. Instead, he sought a "communion with God," but "through earth," that is to say not by rejecting the world, but by actively immersing himself in it, by building, shaping and transforming it. Before starting his creative work he noted in his diary in early 1916: "If I write anything . . . it must be, it seems to me, *in order* to bring together, to reconcile (in a sense) God and the world, that is to say, to show that God eminently fulfils our immanent and pantheistic aspirations."[13] Both the exclusive "communion with earth" and the single-minded "communion with God" remain incomplete for him. A much stronger, more integral and quite new synthesis is attained in what he calls "communion with God through earth."[14]

It took him a lifetime and many years of writing to work out what this synthesis and its corresponding mysticism of action mean. We have to glean from his writings the necessary elements to construct a Teilhardian *theory of mysticism*, but we can also gather many fragments that point to a *different practice of mystical life*, a new kind of spirituality that is life-enhancing and world-transforming.

Pantheistic and monistic experiences are described in his first essay, "Cosmic Life," whereas the experiences of the mystic are expressed as a journey through successive circles of what he calls "the mystical Milieu," a milieu of unifying convergence, of union, communion and integration in which all is made whole: "The mystical Milieu gathers up everything that is made up of energy. Nothing in the world is completely lacking in power, and nothing is rejected, except that which turns its back on the unification of spirit."[15] This is a mysti-

cism of integration and transformation, not a mysticism of
separation, exclusion and rejection. Teilhard does not oppose
sacred and profane mysticism—nature mysticism, soul mysticism and God mysticism—as Zaehner does. He distinguishes
them, but they are part of a continuum. This integral approach also applies to mystical practice. As he wrote in "My
Universe":

> Mystical writers disagree as to whether action must
> precede contemplation as a preparation for it, or whether
> it springs from contemplation, as a superabundant gift
> from God. I must confess that such problems mean
> nothing to me. Whether I am acting or praying, whether
> I am painfully opening up my soul by work, or whether
> God takes possession of it through the passivities that
> come from within or without, I am equally conscious of
> finding unity. Whether I am actively impelled towards
> development by the sensibily perceptible aspirations of
> my nature, or painfully mastered by material contacts,
> or visited by the graces of prayer, in each case I am
> equally moving in the mystical Milieu. *First and fore-
> most,* I am in Christo Jesu; it is only *afterwards* that I am
> acting, or suffering, or contemplating.
>
> If we had to give a more exact name to the mystical
> Milieu we would say that it is a Flesh—for it has all the
> properties the flesh has of palpable domination and
> limitless embrace. When given life by the universal
> Christ, the world is so active and has such warmth, that
> not one of the impressions I receive from it fails to
> "inform" me a little more with God. Like a powerful
> organism, the world transforms me into him who ani-
> mates it. "The bread of the Eucharist," says St. Gregory
> of Nyssa, "is stronger than our flesh; that is why it is the
> bread that assimilates us, and not we the bread, when we
> receive it."[16]

That is a sentiment Teilhard made entirely his own. We have
to recognize the primacy of mystical experience in Teilhard's
reflection on mysticism. His attraction to matter, to nature,
to the cosmos, was based on an innate pantheistic tendency.

This initial pantheistic, cosmic mysticism, which celebrates the beauty and grandeur, the power and energy, the sacredness of the cosmos and all its life, developed into a pan*en*theistic mysticism. The "mystical Milieu" became the "divine milieu" and grew into a mysticism of the noosphere, an energy devoted to knowing and loving, to seeking ever greater unity in all spheres of human experience.

Teilhard's theory of mysticism can be briefly sketched as follows. His passionate interest in all aspects of the human phenomenon made him recognize a movement toward ever greater complexity as well as greater unification in human history and civilization. He pointed to the continuing presence of a mystic sense in human beings, a sense that has found different expressions at different historical times and in different cultures. This mystic sense is itself rooted in the cosmic sense; it finds expression as a sense of unity, a sense of the All that different religions and philosophies have named differently.

Teilhard possessed an acute sense of the plurality and diversity of all living forms. Yet he also sensed their deep affinity and held an overarching, universal vision of the oneness of all that exists. But it is not universalizing in the sense of exclusion, domination or hierachical ordering. On the contrary, it consists in correlating and connecting different elements within a larger whole. His philosophy was not one of essences and substances, but of processes and axes of development, and some axes were more privileged than others in their importance for the overall development of humanity.

He saw the phenomenon of religion as central to the development of the human phenomenon. Within religion he considered the phenomenon of spirituality more important than any other. The center of that, the heart of spirituality, is found in the phenomenon of mysticism, which, in his view, required all the powers of research and critical analysis that we are capable of. Mysticism must be studied just as much as any other phenomenon the human mind investigates. For him all forms of mysticism found their highest expression in a mysticism of action, a dynamic and activating center burning with the fire of love, a mysticism deeply grounded in Christian incarnational theology.

The study of mysticism, as distinct from the lived practice and experience of mysticism, is primarily a new development that emerged during the twentieth century. This is especially true of the comparative study of mysticism. The early part of the twentieth century produced the first surveys of mysticism, the classic studies still read today that highlight the chief characteristics *common* to all mysticisms. These were later followed by more analytical studies, which proposed *different types* of mysticism, especially the distinction between monistic and theistic forms. The work on these typologies was in turn followed by *critical philosophical studies,* which highlight not the similarities, but the differences between mystics, the *diversity and complexity* of forms of mysticism, the *different literary genres* mystics have produced and the philosophical problems posed by *mystical language.* More recently still, much interesting work has been done on the implications of gender differences for the understanding of mysticism and the way it is connected with power, authority and different forms of discourse and knowledge.

As always, Teilhard used a changing, fluid vocabulary when he spoke about mysticism. In the main he distinguished two types of mysticism, a *mysticism of identification or fusion* and a *mysticism of unification or love.* The first is for him almost identical with an apersonal, monistic form of mysticism; the second is a personalist, theistic form. Unfortunately he also described these two forms as "two roads"—the "road of the East" and the "road of the West"—expressions that are bound to create rather misleading associations.[17]

In spite of his great vision of unity and his emphasis on the process of unification, Teilhard was fond of using binary classifications that make the interpretation of his ideas a difficult task. He spoke of "two solutions to the problem of the One and the many," "two roads to unity," "two kinds of pantheism," "two ways of mysticism." It depends on whether a commentator sees such terms as dichotomous, as truly exclusive of and opposed to each other, or whether they are understood as relational and connected with each other, as two poles so to speak, which are held in tension and energize each other.

R. C. Zaehner understood Teilhard's views of mysticism as a confirmation of his own, presented in *Mysticism, Sacred and Profane.*[18] He later described Teilhard as "one of the very few who draw clear distinctions between different types of mysticism."[19] This is only partly correct, however, for Teilhard distinguished the several types of mysticism somewhat differently from Zaehner. Not only did he see pantheism and mysticism as part of a larger continuum of experiences, related to each other rather than fully separate, but he also insisted on the need for a *Christian* pantheism. Christians must learn to perceive and revere the sacredness of matter and the cosmos; the experience of the cosmos is a necessary dimension of human experience that must be integrated into the Christian faith.

The appropriateness of a more integral rather than dichotomous interpretation of Teilhard's types of mysticism becomes clear when other terminology is taken into account. In many letters, notes and essays Teilhard refers to *three different ways* rather than two. He first distinguishes a *via prima* and a *via secunda,* which stand for a basic polarity between a forward and an upward orientation of the human being. The *via prima* refers to a "communion with earth," a nature and social mysticism immersed in and locked into an immanent dimension; the *via secunda* is his "communion with God," a soul and God mysticism that privileges the transcendent dimension in sharp contrast to immanent experiences. Teilhard advocates neither of the two, but a *via tertia,* a third way or direction that represents a *new synthesis* between the forward and the upward.

This is his "communion with God through earth," which he describes as a "new mysticism" where the human being is united with the Absolute, with God, *via the unification of the world.*[20] In this new synthesis, made possible only through the emergence of the modern world, the religious and the mystical are closely interdependent with our knowledge of the natural world and with the construction of our social world, with what he elsewhere calls "building the earth."

In the unpublished diaries of the last years of his life he often refers to this "new mysticism" as a "mysticism of evolution" and a "mysticism of action." In this type of mysticism unification proceeds and unity is achieved through ultra-differentiation. I cannot think of any other writer on mysti-

cism or spirituality who wrestles with similar seriousness and
integrity with contemporary spiritual needs without reduc-
ing them to a primarily inward quest. For Teilhard it is the
integration of the inner and outer as experienced in the modern world that provides the road to a new synthesis and the
possibility of a new mysticism.

Mysticism of Love and Panchristic Mysticism

The importance of such an integration is also brought out
by another consideration. In a brief note of 1951, devoted to
the clarification of the mystical sense,[21] Teilhard speaks of
"two principal ways (and only two—I wonder?)[22] of realizing
oneness . . . tried by the mystics" or rather "two *components*
hitherto merged into one."[23] The first leads to an identification with a *common ground,* to a de-differentiation and
depersonalization, whereas the second seeks the unification
of all elements in a *common focus,* a center. Teilhard speaks
of the first way as a "mysticism WITHOUT LOVE" and sees
the second way as leading to an "ultra-personalizing . . . ul-
tra-differentiating," a unification of all elements that is "the
specific effect of LOVE."[24] In other words, the power of love
expressed through the creative union between persons is seen
as the main differentiating factor. Love is the strongest unifying factor; it is directed outward, toward the other, toward
the world and its problems, toward God.

The fire of love has the greatest power to unite, to transform, to make whole, to heal. For Teilhard a Christian mysticism of love is *the* mysticism par excellence. It has its origin
and ground in the Christian understanding of God as a God
of love whose love is outpoured in creation, incarnation and
redemption. As a Christian, Teilhard could not accept a materialistic or mechanistic understanding of the world. Only a
spiritual view of evolution can do justice to all the phenomena around us, but he also saw humanity reaching a new
psychological state: It is becoming adult and crossing a new
threshold. Not only that, we are standing at the crossroads
where several ways, several options, are open to us. We have
to recognize our full responsibility for shaping the future.

But what future that will be depends to a great extent on

the direction of the road we choose to take. Teilhard maintained that science alone is not enough and does not have all the answers. Science needs the stimulus of religion in terms of spirituality and mysticism, but religion also needs to develop further by taking into account the new contributions that scientific research is making to human consciousness.

His last piece of writing, in March 1955—not long before his death on April 10—was a brief paper, "Research, Work and Adoration."[25] Shortly before, in the same month, he had completed a *summa* of his life's vision and experience in the essay "The Christic,"[26] which he presented as a quintessence of his earlier spiritual works, *The Mass on the World, Le Milieu Divin,* and *The Heart of Matter.* Although it was written in a few weeks, its ideas had been maturing in him for five years or more. In a letter of 1950 he mentioned the idea to a friend: "this extraordinary Christic—I want to live long enough to have time to express it more or less as I now see it taking shape, with an ever-increasing sense of wonder." He asked for the grace to end his life well, but also for the time and opportunity to express once more his "Essential Message, the Essence of my Message."[27]

He had written about the wonder and beauty of the risen Christ many times before; he had prayed to the "ever-greater Christ"; he had included many passages to Jesus in earlier works. For example, in *Le Milieu Divin* he wrote:

> O Jesus . . . Show Yourself to us as the Mighty, the Radiant, the Risen! Come to us once again as the Pantocrator who filled the solitude of the cupolas in the ancient basilicas! Nothing less than this Parousia is needed to counter-balance and dominate in our hearts the glory of the world that is coming into view. And so that we should triumph over the world with You, come to us clothed in the glory of the world.[28]

This passage expresses a love of the world from a perspective of faith where the glory of God is revealed through the wonders of the world. For our more critical sensibility this insight is perhaps too much expressed in a language of triumph and domination. The essay "The Christic" is less triumphant, more humble, more doubtful, but it is an extraordinary testimony to the contagious power and strength of synthesis achieved through the Christian faith in the heart of one twentieth-century person.

The ardor of Teilhard's fundamental vision, his "glorious vision,"[29] its mystical depth and power, are without doubt. He speaks of "the amorization of the universe" and its convergence, of the emergence of Christ and a "christified universe," the consummation of the universe by Christ and of Christ by the universe. He also discusses the possible shape of "the religion of tomorrow." For him, both religion and science are jointly coming of age, thus opening the door for further joint developments, for "a sort of ultra-dimension of Things, in which all differences between Action, Passion (in the sense of being acted upon) and Communion vanish—not by being neutralized but by reaching an explosive climax . . . I saw the Universe becoming amorized and personalized in the very dynamism of its own evolution."[30]

Combining the insights of modern science with those of his Christian faith led him to the intellectual and emotional perception of a cosmic process of convergence and the incarnate presence of God as "christic emergence." Their intimate connection was a tremendous discovery and delight to him so that "when these two spiritual ingredients were brought together, they reacted endlessly upon óne another in a flash of extraordinary brilliance, releasing by their implosion a light so intense that it transfigured (or even 'transsubstantiated') for me the very depths of the World."[31]

But this fundamental vision of integrating science, religion and mysticism, for which he lived and died, was very specific and personal to Teilhard. He anxiously asked himself whether it would remain unique without others to follow? At the end of his life he stood completely alone. He experienced so much pain and loneliness that his friend Pierre Leroy has described this period in Teilhard's life as one of an "inner martyrdom." It is almost tragic how he felt this loneliness and isolation, how he doubted and questioned his own position, his "apparent idiosyncracy."[32] Though still "dazzled" by what he had seen, he asked whether he was the only person to see God and the world in the way he did:

How ... can it be that "when I come down from the
mountain" and in spite of the glorious vision I still retain,
I find that I am so little a better man, so little at peace,
so incapable of expressing in my actions, and thus
adequately communicating to others, the wonderful unity
that I feel encompassing me?

Is there, in fact a Universal Christ, is there a Divine
Milieu?

Or am I, after all, simply the dupe of a mirage in my
own mind?

I often ask myself that question.[33]

He rehearsed for himself the arguments why he continued to
believe in spite of his doubts. Three points are listed as supporting evidence: first, the overall coherence of his views; second, the contagious power of that form of love "in which it
becomes possible to love God 'not only with all one's body and
all one's soul' but with the whole Universe-in-evolution"; and
third, the superiority of his vision compared with the kind of
faith he had been taught in his youth. He saw the faith at the
end of his life in continuity with, but also greatly different
from, his earlier understanding of the Christian faith. His
faith now contained an element of newness, of novelty and
originality, which he gropingly tried to express through a
myriad of new formulations.[34]

Teilhard was deeply concerned to give meaning, direction
and purpose to all human endeavor. More than anything else
he wanted to present the message of the Christian gospel to
a new age, the essential Christian message of an intimate,
incarnate divine presence in the world and the all-transform-
ing power of love. But Christianity as we know it at present
needs reformulation and reshaping. He was asking for a dynamic "neo-Christianity," "a Christianity re-incarnated for a
second time (Christanity, we might say, squared) in the spiritual energies of Matter,"[35] a Christianity reborn "by resolutely
connecting it up to the World in movement." If such a synthesis can be effected, as Teilhard achieved it in his own life,
then Christianity "can display the astonishing power of energizing to the full, by 'amorizing' them, both the powers of
growth and life and the powers of diminishment and death,

at the heart of, and in the process of, the Noogenesis in which we are involved."[36]

Teilhard felt that the idea of evolution, our new understanding of the history of the cosmos and the evolution of life, has created a "new spiritual atmosphere" in the world that invites us to combine the love of God with faith in the world. The fusion of these two forces—of love and faith in a larger, stronger sense—can bring about a powerful chain reaction in the transformation of the world and ourselves. His concluding statement is a powerful one that expresses the strength of a faith tested by doubt, a faith that empowers and inspires. Although still alone at the end of his life, Teilhard nonetheless was able to believe that his ideas were becoming more widely accepted. Countless religious and secular people around him were beginning to think and feel as he did so that he could confidently end his essay "The Christic" with the assurance that the "truth has to appear only once, in one single mind, for it to be impossible for anything ever to prevent it from spreading universally and setting everything ablaze."[37]

The spark of his fire is there till the end. Here speaks the self-authenticating experience of a modern mystic, a voice praising the mysticism of union and love, but expressed in a new language and achieved through a new mode of integration, not just for himself or a few disciples, but for the human community at large. This essay, "The Christic," together with the lines of his litany addressed to the heart of God, the heart of Jesus, the heart of the world, from which I quoted in the last chapter, constitute the final testimony of a great Christian thinker and mystic of today who, just a few months before his death, could say to one of his friends in the very ordinary setting of a busy New York street that he now lived permanently in the presence of God.[38]

To be inspired by Teilhard's example of a deep mystical spirituality, of a life lived in faith and love, is one thing, but what about his ideas? We must go beyond the power of his personal example and ask why he assigns such central significance to the phenomenon of mysticism in human evolution, in the emergent global community. Why does he speak of a *new kind of mysticism*, and what does he mean by it? Why and how does he relate science to mysticism?

A New Mysticism of Action

Teilhard de Chardin is a great Christian mystic, but his mysticism cannot be fully understood or adequately explained without reference to science. If one interprets Teilhard's mystical experiences and thought solely within the traditional categories of mystical religion and personal piety, one easily bypasses the very originality and strength of this new synthesis. His very special integration of modern science with Christian faith could occur only in the modern period, with the rise of modern science, as F. C. Happold has rightly pointed out in his comparative study *Mysticism*. Teilhard's mystic way is one "very different from the *via negativa* of Dionysius and St. John of the Cross. For him union with God was not through withdrawal from the activity of the world but through a dedicated, integrated, and sublimated absorption in it." Happold describes Teilhard's "mysticism of action" as

> springing from the inspiration of a universe seen as moved and com-penetrated by God in the totality of its evolution. And, in its vision of Christ as the All-in-everything, it is also a Christo-mysticism, expanding and reinterpreting the Christo-mysticism of St. Paul.
>
> This is essentially a new type of mysticism, the result of a profound life-long, reconciling meditation on religious and scientific truth; and it is thus of immense relevance and significance for a scientific age such as ours.[39]

Teilhard's approach to and understanding of the universe, of an ordered cosmos, was larger and more comprehensive than simply that of traditional science. However much science had achieved, for Teilhard analysis alone was not enough if it was not also related to synthesis. He criticized science as being often too reductionist, too positivistic, too constricted by little questions without asking bigger ones about direction and meaning, about philosophical and ethical concerns that relate to our responsibilities of being human.

It is Teilhard's personal blending of science, mysticism and poetry that some scientists find hard to accept, whereas theologians cannot easily cope with the cosmic and global dimensions of his thought and his unusual, highly innovative way of extending horizons and boundaries, thus not simply calling into question but sometimes even subtly subverting traditional Christian themes by transforming and reinterpreting them.

Teilhard understood the search for unification of the material, tangible world and the concern for the value of the world as a fundamentally Western preoccupation deeply rooted in the Christian understanding of the incarnation. The full implications of an incarnational approach—the transformation and sanctification of all human and earthly realities—take on an altogether different dimension with the modern discovery and analysis of what these realities are. With our ever-growing scientific knowledge, the limits of the real are forever further pushed back; the horizon of our world and our knowledge of it are forever expanding.

Yet for Teilhard the search for a unitary knowledge in the scientific domain becomes closely related to the mystic search for unification and union in the religious domain. This interrelated quest for greater oneness makes him speak of a "new mysticism" where unification is achieved through ultra-differentiation, where diversity is sustained and affirmed through complexity. He applied the concept of mysticism in an analogous way to science itself, as is evident from such essays as "The Mysticism of Science" (1939)[40] and "The Religious Value of Research" (1947).[41] When one examines his thought one realizes that, seen from a contemporary perspective, his work is already part of a postenlightenment project that critiques the one-sided use of rationality and the mechanistic and positivistic philosophies of science. Teilhard sees the tremendous drive of modern science on the one hand as a "mysticism of discovery," an energy of an almost religious nature, a sacred pursuit showing disinterested passion and carried forward by a "hope in a limitless future."[42] But on the other hand much of this energy is "still lost in the abyss of armaments and war," as he wrote in 1939. He felt even then that the pillars of positivism and mechanism were collapsing and the ruins of materialism were in evidence all around us.

While most people see the modern conflict between science and religion as a conflict between reason and faith, Teilhard speaks of it as a struggle between two mysticisms for the mastery of the human heart. He was convinced that the religion of science was dead. We need a new mysticism:

> Fundamentally no mysticism can live without love. The religion of science believed that it had found a faith, a hope. It has died by excluding Christian love . . .
>
> In order to sustain and extend the huge, invincible and legitimate effort of research in which the vital weight of human activity is at present engaged, a faith, a mysticism is necessary . . . religion is the soul biologically necessary for the future of science. Humanity is no longer imaginable without science. But no more science is possible without some religion to animate it. Christianity is an exemplary form of the religion of science. Must I add that it is the necessary form . . . the Christian scientist seems to everyone the best situated and the best prepared to develop in himself and foster around him the new human type . . . : the seeker who devotes himself, ultimately through love, to the labours of discovery. No longer a worshipper of the world but of something greater than the world, through and beyond the world in progress. Not the proud and cold Titan, but Jacob passionately wrestling with God.[43]

After the Second World War he spoke about the vital function of historical and experimental research, as vital to the continuing life of the human community as are nutrition and reproduction. Our age is characterized not only by the social rise of the masses, but also by the "rise of research," the passion for knowledge and mastery. From a biological perspective he judged the expansion and intensification of research in all fields as a new growth, as "evolution *in its hominised phase*" at a period when humanity has reached adulthood and finds itself compelled to take control of the evolution of life on earth. In this new stage "research is the actual expression . . . of this evolutionary effort . . . not simply to continue to exist, but to exist more fully; not simply to survive but irreversibly to 'super-live.' "[44] He was speaking here to his Jesuit confrères about the importance of research for them, and he asked why they share in it so fully and permeate it with their faith and love for Christ. He answered his own question by saying that

> research is the form in which the creative power of God is hidden and operates the most intensely. Through our research, new being, a further increase in consciousness, emerges in the world. This new creation would, surely, remain incomplete, "unlivable," if it were not included as manifestly as possible . . . among the forms assumed by an Incarnation and Redemption, each a complement of the other. Every fruit of research is by its nature, essentially, ontologically, Christifiable ("christifiabilis" and "christificandus") so that the world may have complete existence in every part of it. The place for us priests, then, is precisely there, at the point from which all truth and all new power emerges: so that Christ may inform every growth, through man, of the universe in movement.[45]

He recognized that this was a truly *theological* perspective on research. He also knew that at the same time it can be psychologically very satisfying and enriching to develop a meaningful discourse about science and religion, about religion, science and mysticism, which are always so closely intertwined in his thought. He assigns central significance to a new "mysticism of action," which is a mysticism of unification, transformation and sanctification where holiness is understood as wholeness. His own life was a life of action, work, prayer and meditation that brought together in a mystical vision the immersion in a vast "cosmic milieu," enlarged through the encounter with a rich, diverse "human milieu." Both together made possible a continuous participation and communion with a diaphanous "divine milieu" that shines through and transforms all realities.

In the original sense of the French meaning of "milieu," the "divine milieu" refers both to a center point and a sphere, a total environment in which we are all immersed if we can but

MYSTICISM-IN-ACTION   **97**

perceive it. Such mystical "seeing" with the eyes of faith is capable of transforming and transfiguring all human experiences. In this sense Teilhard's "seeing" is more than a phenomenological method because his work and thought are suffused with a particular mystical spirituality. He is an exemplar not only of lifelong research and action, but of a lifelong meditation on religious and scientific truth. Bringing these different worlds of experience together was his specific milieu wherein he breathed and lived. This is what he meant when he spoke of the divinization of our activities and the divinization of our passivities—that all that we are, all we do and all we suffer, can be transformed into a spiritual activity, thereby deeply transforming its meaning by giving it value and purpose.

Teilhard wanted to develop a concretely rooted spirituality, closely linked to our experience of the earth and its peoples, rooted in nature, body and community. His emphasis is on *creative transformation* at all levels, affecting our work, our thoughts, our prayer, our society, our whole world, a transformation brought about by the powers of spirit, which are structurally related to the powers of matter, not dualistically separate from them. However concretely grounded and fed by the powers of matter, of the earth, of life, such a spirituality must be animated by the dynamics of love, which itself has cosmic roots. His mysticism is an experience and vision that expresses itself in action, in taking on full responsibility for one's own life and that of the world by responding to the exciting challenge of living up to what it means to be fully human.

Teilhard's understanding of mysticism cannot be assessed solely by reference to the mystics of the past since his own interpretation of mysticism is strongly oriented toward the present and the future, and is also basically evaluative. The mysticism of identification and that of unification are not simply two equivalent types; rather, one of the two—the type centered on the powers of love—is privileged as a more developed, fuller, richer kind of mysticism. At an interfaith meeting held in Paris in 1948 Teilhard is reported to have said:

I believe the mystical is less different, less separated from the rational than one says, but I finally also believe that the whole problem which the world, and we in particular, are presently facing is a problem of faith . . .

I have the weakness to believe that the West has a very strong latent mysticism, underlying, not made explicit yet, but at least as strong as Eastern mysticism.

If the Western group were really able to express in a new manner, or to renew, that mysticism of the West of which I once spoke, I think that would be something much more powerful than even dialogue, for it would make a faith appear within humankind, a mysticism which does not yet exist.[46]

Perhaps it is Teilhard's main achievement to have sought a new formulation for such a mysticism rooted in the Christian doctrines of creation and incarnation, but experienced and expressed in a new manner. At the same time he also stressed the need for a deep transformation of the Christian tradition when he wrote: "Christianity has only a chance to survive . . . if it shows itself capable . . . to activate to a maximum in the human being 'the energy of self-evolution,' i.e., if it is successful . . . not only in 'amorising' the world but in valuing it more highly than any other form of religion."[47] What is needed is a "Christianity faithfully extended to its utmost limit,"[48] that is a Christianity that surpasses itself. Teilhard was looking for something "trans-Christian" in theology and mysticism,[49] for a "new mysticism, at once fully human and fully Christian" that will supply us with a new energy for which "we have as yet *no name.*"[50]

Teilhard de Chardin not only thought about mysticism, he also lived it. We have in Teilhard a splendid example of a modern Christian mystic who stated with great humility that he had been "visited by the graces of prayer"[51] and the presence of God in the midst of today's world. But his ideas on mysticism have sometimes been written off as of no interest to the scholar and phenomenologist of religion. I strongly dispute this. While he does not provide us with a systematic "grand theory" on mysticism, his works contain many seminal ideas that can contribute important insights to the debates on mysticism and spirituality, as well as those on science and religion.

And anyone seriously concerned with the future of religion in modern society must be open to reflections on the future of mysticism. Teilhard considered mysticism not only as a resource of the past, of merely historical interest, but as of vital importance for the present and future life of humankind. He also invited a critical-constructive approach to the study of mysticism, to this extraordinarily powerful phenomenon in human history and life—the greatest source of human energy, which must be harnessed for the benefit of the whole human community, for a new mysticism-in-action provides one of the most empowering visions to foster faith, love and greater union among all the peoples of the earth.

CHAPTER SIX

Interfaith Dialogue and Christian Spirituality

The Spiritual Contribution of World Faiths

ᏩᎻᏪᎧ

Our world is a world shaped by science and technology, by global interdependencies, by diverse and often oppressive political and industrial power structures. It is a world of growing democracies swept by immense waves of human hopes and expectations. But it is also a world of much dissension and strife, of violence, conflict and savage wars, of militarism and torture, hunger and poverty, environmental damage and disaster. There exist racial and religious discrimination, communal hatred and much personal suffering and unhappiness around the globe. The widespread existence of religious diversity frequently contributes additional disagreement and dissension, which often exacerbate existing economic and political conflicts.

The Christian faith is present everywhere in the world today, but is only one faith among many, however numerous its adherents. If we are honest and realistic we must ask ourselves: What is the contribution, importance and validity of Christian faith and practice for people in search of anwers to so many burning questions?

Characterized by an empowering, life-giving vision, there exist great strength, transformative potential and healing power in Christian faith and spirituality, but there is also much room for critical self-examination and reflection. A creative renewal is needed, a reappraisal of what is at the center of the Christian tradition. This center can be summed up as "Seeing Christ in all things and all things in Christ," as many Christians have done through many generations. Yet we have to express this experience today in forms and language different from those of the past so that this profound message makes full sense to us and our time. I have argued in this book that among the abundant resources available for Christian renewal one of the most powerful exists in the much neglected work of the French Jesuit and mystic Pierre Teilhard de Chardin.

The previous chapters dealt with the contemporary understanding of spirituality; with Teilhard de Chardin's own religious experience, faith and spiritual vision; with some central themes of his work, such as his emphasis on spirituality and human energy resources, his understanding of God's presence in the world and in Christ; and with his experience and interpretation of mysticism. The present chapter deals with the theme of Christian spirituality and interfaith dialogue.

Religious pluralism is here to stay, but what do we do with it? How can a greater awareness and acknowledgment of religious differences be used as an opportunity to widen the doors and windows of our minds, so that we learn to appreciate the faiths of others and overcome dividing differences by the transforming powers of understanding and love? Faced with religious pluralism and an extraordinary diversity of beliefs and spiritualities, we have to ask ourselves what the deeper meaning of this situation can possibly be. How can we not only discern the existence of diversity, but also become aware of the spiritual contribution the world faiths, each in its own way and also all together, can make in solving some of our contemporary problems, not least the problem of constructing a meaningful and dignified human life for more people on the planet?

Many know the English hymn "There's a Wideness in God's Mercy like the Wideness of the Sea." It contains insights that are appropriate to the theme of religious pluralism and interfaith dialogue. The sea, the ocean, is an image often found in religious and mystical literature, where it can refer to the ocean of God's being and love. But the image of the ocean is also used in connection with religious diversity, in the sense that different religions are seen as different rivers, each following a different course, but all ending up in one and the same ocean, which is their common goal and ultimate home, however understood.

As the hymn so clearly states: "The love of God is broader than the measure of man's mind . . . But we make his love too narrow by false limits of our own; and we magnify his strictness with a zeal he will not own." Apart from the exclusively male reference to God's ultimate being and love, this verse might well serve as a motto, if not a warning, for much of current interreligious encounter and dialogue, where our ways of thinking are often far too narrow and exclusive. We have to think in larger, more imaginative terms in order to develop the necessary intellectual, spiritual and existential resources for transforming ourselves and the social and political world around us. Only then will we be able to acknowledge religious diversity as a source of growth and strength rather than of division and strife.

I want to reflect on interfaith dialogue in today's world and link our contemporary situation to Teilhard de Chardin's earlier experience of religious diversity, and to his reflections on the religiously plural context of the modern world. I also want to ask how spirituality and interfaith dialogue relate to each other.

Interfaith Dialogue in Today's World

The great faith traditions of the world are not isolated, fortified territories of an exclusive kind, but homes of the spirit where our whole being can be nurtured and strengthened. If we do not look at religions exclusively from the outside, seeing nothing more than their defective institutional settings and structures, but instead discover their deeper spiritual resources, we become aware that all the spiritual traditions together present us with an immensely rich, global heritage that belongs to all of humankind. It is part of human cultural capital, but it also much more—a rich revelation of an inexhaustible divine ocean of love, compassion and mercy, and of the possibility of human dignity and wholeness, of greatness and glorification. We can also see that the ethical codes of different faiths can help us to construct what has been called a "global ethic" for conflict resolution, for overcoming violence, poverty and inequality, and for learning the art of peace-making.

Our world needs a "dialogical imperative," that is to say the urgent and necessary command to promote dialogue above all else. This requires the often difficult acceptance of difference and diversity, attentive listening to others, sharing and healing differences and mutually enriching growth. Dialogue is about voices of difference, about different moods and experiences, about different life worlds, about different ways of living and experiencing, different ways of knowing, thinking, feeling and acting. The human being has an inborn intentionality for communication and relationships, but the range for realizing this potential has grown exponentially in today's world.

True dialogue is an art which must be learned. The requirements for dialogue between people of different faiths go far beyond those of ordinary day-to-day conversation and human contact. Much has been written on the conditions, methods and problems of interfaith communication, but there can be no doubt that dialogical concerns have opened up new worlds to us. Numerically speaking, the believers of different faiths engaged in the experimental and experiential process of dialoguing are still very, very few. There were early individual pioneers and path-finders, followed by such organizations as the World Congress of Faiths, founded in 1936 by Sir Francis Younghusband in London,[1] and the subsequent efforts of the Temple of Understanding, the World Council of Churches' Subunit "Dialogue with People of Living Faiths and Ideologies," and the Roman Catholic initiatives in interfaith dialogue encouraged since the Second Vatican Council. More recently still there is the establishment of the new International Interfaith Centre in Oxford. In addition there have been many individuals and groups fostering dialogue at the grass-roots level. Thus the interfaith movement, as it is sometimes called, has gained considerable momentum since its beginning, which is often dated to the year 1893 when the first World's Parliament of Religions was held in Chicago.[2]

This reminds us clearly, if a reminder is necessary, that interfaith dialogue initiatives are primarily a feature of modernity in the West. They were originally linked to the Western expansion of mind and occurred within a colonial and missionary context, whether in India, China, Japan, North Africa or the Middle East.[3] It was in colonized countries, opened up to Christian missions, that Christians first encountered religious diversity and were existentially and intellectually challenged to reflect on the significance of profound religious differences. This earlier history still affects some of the dynamic patterns of interfaith dialogue today, although many contemporary "dialogicians" may not be fully aware of this colonial and missionary heritage.

However, the end of colonial rule and of Christian missions from a position of superiority has long given way to encounter in the context of an *equal partnership in dialogue*. The contemporary practice of dialogue is itself an event of religious significance, and that is why it is particularly important for the theme of spirituality. But the full equality and mutuality of all partners in dialogue can be practiced only in a fully democratic and secular society.

I would argue that dialogue, as we understand and promote it today, is dependent on the condition of secularity as a positive value. I do not mean secularism as a pervasive, militant ideology, but secularity as the necessary space for religious and political freedom where religious and spiritual values can be explored without threat to one's integrity, one's job or one's life. This requirement is part of the increased complexity we have to negotiate today. In order to explore the different positions of faith in relation to each other, we need to be grounded in a space of freedom not predetermined by prior positioning.

You may well ask what all this has to do with Teilhard de Chardin, who was such an ardent Christian. I would like to show that in most of his writings the very *ardor* of his faith is proportionate to the *openness* of this faith. We can see in his life and thought the recognition of otherness, however hard at times, and the adventurous questioning of different faiths and their significance for the understanding of his own. This self-reflexive questioning outweighs the opposite attitude, also present, of judging other faiths in the light of his own. Such judgment can be painful and mistaken at times, but the primary motivation for Teilhard's reflections on other faiths was nonetheless the search for a powerful spiritual renewal, especially the renewal of Christianity in the West. Let us therefore consider his contacts with people from different faiths.

Teilhard's Experience of Religious Diversity

Teilhard's family background from a traditional French aristocratic line in the Auvergne and his Jesuit training of many years meant that he initially experienced a very uniform religious life-world, entirely shaped by traditional Roman Catholic beliefs and practices. But he was also aware of a strong attraction to a very different civilization and culture, that of China. His curiosity and interest were first awakened through the travels of his older brother, and later through the religious vocation of his older sister, who went to work among the poor in Shanghai toward the end of the first decade of the present century.

Teilhard himself experienced another culture and religion firsthand through being sent to teach in a Jesuit college in Cairo between 1905 and 1908. Many of his pupils came from Muslim families, and with some of them he maintained considerable contact in later years. In Egypt he had an opportunity, although not always as much as one might wish, to learn something about ancient Egyptian culture, about contemporary Islam in a North African setting and about eastern Christianity in its Orthodox and Coptic forms. His mystical experiences and his reading on mysticism gave him a general interest in Eastern religions, although this was never developed in great depth or detail.

But in later years his long stay in China and his extensive travels in the East made him encounter Buddhism, Confucianism and certain forms of Islam in China, Hinduism in India, Burmese and Sri Lankan Buddhism, Indonesian Islam and expressions of Tibetan Buddhism in Mongolia and other parts of Central Asia. This is certainly quite a diverse and impressive list of encounters that not many people can match even today. Apart from missionaries working overseas, there were probably not many Christian priests or theologians during the earlier part of the twentieth century who came into living contact with so many religiously diverse groups of people. In addition Teilhard had several close friends who were Jewish, and he also was in regular contact with lapsed Catholics, atheists and communists.

Given this rich experiential background, how did he conceptualize religious pluralism and get personally involved in interfaith dialogue?

It is particularly his first-hand contact with eastern societies and religions that made him unusually open to, reflective on and critical of the state of religion in the contemporary world. I have written about Teilhard's experience and knowledge of Eastern religions at great length elsewhere.[4] Here I simply want to explain how his passionate interest in mysticism and spirituality shaped all his questions and made him look for comparisons and structural correlations among what he called the "living branches" of religions or the "active currents of faith." These thoughts are scattered across numerous essays, but when taken together and systematically analyzed they add up to quite an interesting theory about religion, including reflections on religious pluralism that, in turn, are rooted in some of his own practical activities in interfaith encounter and dialogue.

Teilhard's Reflection on Religious Pluralism and His Activities in Interfaith Dialogue

Teilhard's theory of religious pluralism is not a theory arrived at by logical deduction and abstract intellectual synthesis in the traditional mode of philosophy, theology or even the phenomenology of religion. On the contrary, his thinking is deeply rooted in the *biodiversity of life* as a planetary phenomenon, shaped by birth and development. In an evolutionary context diversity is strength; reduction to uniformity and overspecialization lead to extinction of species. Religions are ultimately part of the diversity of life, central to what we might call the *noospheric diversity* of human life.

Teilhard looks at religious diversity historically and biologically, not theologically in terms of revelation or the significance of other religions for Christian theology. Ultimately he is interested in the *spiritual significance of religious diversity*, but phenomenologically speaking, different religious ways of life are part of the different cultures and civilizations that all through history have evolved around the globe. But their development during earlier historical periods occurred in different geographical areas, mostly in isolation from each other, or in limited contact with or opposition to each other. Teilhard now perceives the growth of religions as occurring in a state of global expansion where contacts are far more numerous than in earlier eras of human history and the possibilities for greater collaboration and reflection together are greatly intensified in comparison with the past.

He speaks of the great "rivers," "currents" or different "branches" of religion, images drawn from the organic world of nature. These currents have different characteristics and orientations, but given the process character of both the universe and the human being, we are now experiencing a *change of epoch* and a *change of the scale of time,* which point to a newly emerging, different civilization that is universal and global in a new sense.

In his essay "Christianity in the World," written in 1933, Teilhard speaks of the "biological function" of religion in the further evolution of the human community. Religion provides "a foundation for morality," "a dominating principle of order," and an axis of movement, "something of supreme value, to create, to hold in awe, or to love." But religion itself must "grow greater and more clearly defined in step with . . . and in the same degree" as humanity.[5] For Teilhard humankind today "is undecided and distressed, at the very peak of its power, because it has not defined its spiritual pole. It lacks religion."[6]

The urgent question now is, whether religions can give meaning to this "change of epoch," whether they can respond creatively to a historically new situation. In our present situation all religious ideas and practices are "put to the test" of how far they can provide seeds for development and renewal. Teilhard assesses religions from a dynamic, developmental perspective that encourages research, effort and a religion of action.

How far are religions closed or open systems? There can

be no encounter between systems that are closed to each other, and a mere peaceful coexistence of religions, however worthwhile an aim, is not enough. There must be a further evolution of religion itself. The change of age and direction in contemporary culture means that traditional religious currents have to react to similar sets of problems. This requires that they must all clarify their fundamental orientation, and this common task will draw them more closely together. For Teilhard the need for clarification arose through the encounter between religions and the modern world. All religions are now faced with similar questions, with the same problems. Answers have to be found to such fundamental issues as "God and his transcendence; the world and its value; the individual and the importance of the person; mankind and social requirements."[7] The common problems religions now have to wrestle with also include some of the great ethical issues articulated in the *Declaration Toward a Global Ethic,* announced at the 1993 Parliament of the World's Religions in Chicago.[8]

For Teilhard it was abundantly clear that new relations are needed between the different religions because of the new context in which we live. The development of such new relations will affect individuals and communities in a new way. It is ultimately a particular kind of spirituality and mysticism that matters most because he considered a rightly understood spirituality the very center of religion. The possibility of a life-affirming and life-transforming spirituality is closely related to the spark of fire, the power to feed the zest for life, the energizing forces of the Spirit that only religion can transmit.

How far does any *particular religion* contribute its own, special solution to the modern religious problem?[9] Does Christianity, or Judaism, Islam, Hinduism or Buddhism for that matter, speak meaningfully to the present crisis in civilization, to the fundamental moral and ethical problems of our time?

Teilhard's questions and comparisons are always made from a Christian point of view, but his is not a narrowly denominational or dogmatic perspective, but rather a universalist, inclusive one, concerned with a more adequate and richer spirituality for the human community.

In the relatively few passages where Teilhard speaks about Islam—to mention just one example here—he recognizes the close interrelationship between the human being and nature existing in Islam, its recognition of the organic nature of society, its cosmic sense of mystical oneness found in the great Sufis and, as the greatest, strongest feature of Islam, its affirmative celebration of the existence and greatness of God. But writing in a critical vein, as he was wont to do of all religions, Teilhard also mentions the fixation and stagnation of traditional Islam whose great God seems to have been made ineffective and sterile. However, he also recognized the signs of an energizing renascence of Islam in the contemporary world.[10] Teilhard always sided with the modernists and progressives of any religion, never with the traditionalists. It was a *Neo*-Christianity, but also a *Neo*-Buddhism and a *Neo*-Hinduism, and other reform movements that took the modern world seriously, that in his view could perhaps show us a spiritually helpful and enriching way forward.

It is from these premises that he envisaged a "convergence" of religions, a "confluence" of the different currents, not in the sense of a merger, a drowning in the same ocean with the loss of historical individuality and distinctiveness, but a further meaningful development together in relationship with each other, whose outcome we cannot yet predict. This is a unitive, yet diversified pluralism, not a chaotic and totally unrelated plurality of religions.

It is not misplaced to call Teilhard one of the early pioneers of interfaith dialogue, for he explicitly supported and took part in interfaith activities from 1946 onward, after his return to Paris from China. It was then that a group of French scholars and intellectuals interested in Eastern religions got together to found *Le Congrès Universel des Croyants,* later simply called *Union des Croyants* or "Association of Believers," which was loosely affiliated with the World Congress of Faiths in London.

Officially founded in 1947, the *Union des Croyants* did not have a formal membership, but it provided a useful field of activities for Teilhard in Paris between the years 1947 and 1951. Here were the well-known Islamicist Louis Massignon, the orientalist Jacques Bacot, René Grousset, the director of the *Musée Cernuschi,* and other staff working at the oriental museum, *Musée Guimet*, who came together to meet regularly with people of different faiths in order to promote what today would be called interreligious dialogue. Teilhard saw it as an opportunity to encourage greater unity and understanding, and he was very keen to support these developments. Although not an official committee member, he is said to have been present at many meetings that included, among others, an Iranian Sufi, a Confucian, the Hindu Swami Siddheswarananda from the Ramakrishna Mission, and the French philosophers Étienne Gilson, Gabriel Marcel and Edouard Le Roy, with whom Teilhard had closely collaborated in the twenties.

According to Jacques Bacot, Teilhard was often present as a "guest and adviser who contributed all his ardour," his enthusiasm and support for the work of the association. Altogether one can identify three specific essays and three shorter, unpublished papers that Teilhard wrote between 1947 and 1950 especially for the *Union des Croyants*.[11] I would like to quote a few passages and mention some key ideas.[12]

First of all, it seems significant that Teilhard was chosen to give the inaugural address for the foundation of the *Union des Croyants*. Due to difficulties with his own church authorities, he was not allowed to lecture in public. His address was therefore read by René Grousset. Entitled "Faith in Man," Teilhard's inaugural address is based on the idea that people of different faiths and world views can, in spite of their differences, come together through their shared faith in the value of the human being. Believers of different faiths can cooperate in building together a common future. They can respond constructively to our current spiritual crisis, which Teilhard sees as directly linked to the present awakening and transformation of human consciousness. This transformation is closely linked to the essentially modern experience of collectivity, what we might call the process of globalization, and the possibility of an organic, interdependent future for all of humankind. Teilhard states:

> A tendency towards unification is everywhere manifest, and especially in the different branches of religion. We are looking for something that will draw us together,

below or above the level of that which divides . . . Not through external pressure but only from an inward impulse can the unity of Mankind endure and grow . . .

We may say that faith in Man . . . shows itself upon examination to be the general atmosphere in which the higher, more elaborated forms of faith which we all hold in one way or another may best (indeed *can only*) grow and come together . . .

No one can doubt that we are all more or less affected by this elementary, primordial faith. Should we otherwise truly belong to our time? I have said that the spirit has only one summit. But it has also only one basis. Let us look well and we shall find that our Faith in God, detached as it may be, sublimates in us a rising tide of human aspirations. It is to this original sap that we must return if we wish to communicate with the brothers with whom we seek to be united.[13]

In other, earlier texts Teilhard spoke of the necessary integration of two kinds of faiths—a faith in God ahead and a faith in God above, combining the immanent God of evolution with the idea of a transcendent God. In this text for the *Union des Croyants*, addressed to people of different faiths and none, he emphasized faith in the human being, the world, the future as a common basis for a humanity seeking the spirit at its summit. We might say today that in spite of our religious differences we can be collaborative partners working for justice and peace, and a better world for all, and that such a development includes an implicit life-sustaining and energizing spirituality.

On another occasion, in discussion with Louis Massignon and Gabriel Marcel, Teilhard again stressed the importance of and the need for a faith, but also the necessity to recognize the right to a faith in others as well as the need to collaborate with those who do not adhere to any particular faith at all. He recognized a movement of coming together, of convergence, that must include contributions from people of all faiths. But he was also critically aware that the West at present "has not yet found its formula of faith" to deal with the huge problems of our contemporary situation. He said during this discussion that maybe a faith and mysticism that do not exist at present will develop in the human community.[14]

Among all the papers written for the *Union des Croyants*, the one entitled *Le goût de vivre* ("The Zest for Living") deals most explicitly with the role of religions in the contemporary world. Dated December 1950, it emphasizes the important contribution that religions make to the development of the human community. So what can we now expect from a *combined* effort of all religions together?

During the nineteenth century it was often fervently, though wrongly, believed that the age of religions had passed. But although science has had a profound influence on refashioning religious beliefs and practices, it has not destroyed religion as the greatest source of mental and spiritual energy for human beings. Far from being bygone, the era not of *religions* but of *religion* is only beginning, for Teilhard envisaged an increase rather than a decrease in the "reserves of faith." This may come as a surprise to some, but this prediction is related to the recognition of the need for a new spirituality— a spirituality that corresponds to our new historical situation and to the emergence of a new consciousness in the human community:

> What is most vitally necessary to the thinking earth is a faith—and a great faith—and ever more faith . . .
>
> A certain pessimism around us repeats that our world sinks into atheism. Instead, should one not rather say that what it is suffering from is *unsatisfied theism*? You say, men do not want God any longer. Are you quite sure that what they are rejecting is *not* simply the image of a God who is too small to nourish in us that interest to go on living and to live on a higher plane to which, in the end, one must relate the need for adoration?[15]

Teilhard criticized any religion whose spirituality is concerned only with the individual. A spirituality focused on the individual is much too narrow and confined. Instead he was seeking "a religion for humanity and the earth" in which some of the best insights of traditional faith would be combined with a newborn faith in our world today. He quite rightly asked

whether, when taking such a position, it might not be better
to reject all traditional creeds and adopt instead a completely new, evolutionary faith based on the modern "sense of man"
—perhaps "the sort of religion that has been foretold with
such warmth and brilliance by my friend Julian Huxley: to
which he has given the name of 'evolutionary humanism.' "[16]
Teilhard seriously considered this solution, but rejected it not
only because he doubted that present human consciousness
and planetary co-reflection would really be capable of developing this kind of religion, but even more because of the rich
spiritual heritage available in all living religions. These precious elements cannot be replaced and must be preserved:

> There can be no doubt that in each of the great religious
> branches that cover the world at this moment, a certain
> spiritual attitude and vision which have been produced
> by centuries of experience are preserved and continued;
> these are as indispensable and irreplaceable for the
> integrity of a total terrestrial religious consciousness as
> the various "racial" components.[17]

This, however, is not all. What is carried along by the various
currents of faith that are still active on earth, working in
their incommunicable core, is no longer only the irreplaceable elements of a certain complete image of the universe.
"Very much more even than *fragments of vision*, it is *experiences of contact* with a supreme Inexpressible which they preserve and pass on."[18]

Note Teilhard's reference to "the integrity of a total terres-
trial religious consciousness," or what we might call "global
consciousness," in this passage. We need to be aware of, acknowledge and respect the very diversity of faiths, and yet
we must see this diversity in a much larger framework as
being interconnected and belonging together in a humanity
that wants to understand itself as one. For Teilhard the active currents of faiths are indispensable for feeding and main-
taining the human zest for life. In his words, when we are
"sustained and guided by the tradition of the great human
mysticisms, we succeed, through contemplation and prayer,
in entering directly into receptive communication with the

very source of all inner striving."[19] That is to say, people of faith, people of prayer and spiritual practice, people who are seekers and pilgrims on the path of life, can meet, share and walk together respecting each other's spiritual heritage and treasures.

To develop these ideas further, what spirituality might we then expect from interfaith dialogue? How is Christian spirituality influenced and transformed by dialogue with people from other faiths? What is the spiritual contribution of world faiths to our own spirituality?

Spirituality and Interfaith Dialogue

The existence of religious pluralism and interfaith dialogue has been far more reflected upon philosophically and theologically than from the perspective of spirituality. Much of what is referred to as the Christian theology of religions concerns itself with comparative investigations of the understanding of God, revelation, salvation, scriptures, the uniqueness and universality of Christianity or the nature of the church, rather than spiritual growth and transformation. But spiritual awakening and renewal take place when people share in interfaith worship or meet in retreats or, more often, reflect in dialogue together on the spiritual meaning of their beliefs and practices, or share in depth some of the experiences and struggles of their lives.

Much spiritual awakening and deepening occurs in particular dialogues between particular people—between Buddhists and Christians, or Jews, Christians and Muslims, or between Christians and Hindus, and so on. But this is not the place to explore such specific encounters; I can only offer some general reflections on the plurality of religions, interfaith dialogue and newly developing spiritualities.

Many traditional Christians in the West are suspicious of or skeptical about dialogue. They defend traditional Christianity without sufficient attention to the enriching aspects of religious and cultural pluralism. With the presence of so many different Eastern religions and new religious movements in our midst, some Western people retreat into an unnecessarily narrow, defensive position, almost fearing an invasion by alien creeds. This fear is part of the fear of "otherness" that may at first appear as a barrier, a stumbling block to us. But it is important, in fact essential, to nurture an openness and will to seek deeper understanding, respect for and acceptance of otherness around us. We all need to learn, and we need to teach our children and youth, to appreciate otherness and that includes the otherness of spiritual paths, practices and goals.

The depth, seriousness and integrity of authentic spirituality can be tested. Such authentic spirituality is not an individualistic, interiorizing, other-worldly spirituality or a spirituality that is dualistic, reductionist and life-denying. On the contrary, true spirituality is holistic, life-celebrating and affirming; it is embedded in communal praxis, in a cumulative tradition from which individual persons are fed and nourished. As the Indian theologian Samuel Rayan has said: "Spiritual life is human life, the whole of human life inspired and led by the Spirit, the energizing presence and activity of God . . . The Spirit is the breath of God by which we breathe. It is the divine sea of life in which we live and move and have our being."[20]

Rayan understands such spirituality as linked to *openness* and *response-ability,* responsibility not as accountability but taken as the ability to respond to the many different dimensions of reality, to different things, events and people. This includes the ability to respond to the realities of other faiths and their spiritual horizons and insights. We have to cultivate a deep inner awareness to develop such openness. Only then can we discover the mysteries, meanings and revelatory moments of other faiths where the power of the Spirit breaks through again and again into the continuing stream of our historical brokenness and becoming.

In Samuel Rayan's view, the "more open we are, the more spiritual" we are; "the more realities to which we are open, the greater the spirituality; the greater the depths and the profounder the meanings of reality to which we are open, the more authentic the spirituality."[21] Spirituality has also been described as the "Godwardness of life" whereby we see God in all things and all things in God. For the Christian this means to see all things through the flesh of God, through

God's incarnation in the world through Christ, who in an all-inclusive, cosmic sense gathers all things within him. The open arms of Christ on the cross and his open heart pierced by the wounds of the world can be seen as an immense, cosmic outflowing and gathering-in, open to all realities, to all peoples, to all faiths in the embrace of love and the act of feeding. For the Christian this is the center.

People of other faiths will be oriented toward other centers and other ways of approaching the depths of the Spirit. But are we not all seeking a dimension that gives our life deeper meaning and significance, an attitude that honors, praises and adores something and Someone greater than ourselves? Do we not all need a spirituality that "constructs and nurtures what makes for a fuller life, for finer humanity, and for a new earth?"[22]

The encounter with people of other faiths and the serious engagement in interfaith dialogue can be experienced as an appeal, an invitation, a challenge, a marvelous opportunity to take otherness seriously and appreciate differences. Interfaith dialogue makes us first of all discover the pluralism of spiritualities themselves—and that can be a sobering, difficult, but also strengthening discovery. It makes us find new paths and lands of the mind and soul; it makes us experience different traces and touches of the Spirit, which can spiritually uplift and strengthen us. The spirituality of interfaith dialogue can give us a new freshness with which to marvel at the riches of creation.

The spiritual probing of religious pluralism and the drinking from each other's spiritual streams and wells may well be the great spiritual event of our time, full of significance for our future well-being. It is for this reason that some speak of a "newly emerging spirituality" today. This is what I want to explore further in the next two chapters, which will deal with the theme of spirituality among third-world theologians, especially women theologians, and also with spirituality and ecology. Ultimately all these themes come together in the wholeness of Christ in which all Christian spirituality finds its true heart and center—but it is a Christ who also walks on other roads than the ones we have been traditionally taught to recognize.

CHAPTER SEVEN

Third World Theology and the Voices of Women

The Spiritual Significance of Otherness

ᏮᎢᏢᎵᎤ

The renewal of Christian spirituality cannot be achieved by simply retrieving spiritual treasures of the past. It has to be undertaken in engaged dialogue with the present. Spiritual wisdom of the past becomes alive and meaningful only if it has a bearing on the feeling, suffering and hopes of people today. The last chapter looked at the spiritual significance of interfaith dialogue and the importance of religious pluralism for the contemporary transformation of spirituality. This chapter looks at sources for Christian renewal that can be found in Third World theology and the newly emerging spiritualities of Third World women.

The "Third World" is a problematic word, often unsuitable, and unsatisfactory at best. Yet I retain it. So many people, not least theologians, use it as a self-description. Reference to the Third World acts as a significant marker; it points to a different experience from that of people living in the West or the northern part of the globe.

The Third World is such a different world from our own. In fact, it consists of many multilayered worlds whose otherness is often difficult to comprehend. My question is, what is the spiritual significance of this "otherness" for us, for Christians in the First World, for the renewal of Christian spirituality today? To answer this let us first briefly reflect on the meaning of "the other."

117

Reflecting on "the Other"

The idea of the "other" occupies such a dominant place in contemporary intellectual debate that one could easily believe that no one had ever given thought to the otherness of others before. But do we not have many insights about the stranger, the enemy, the unknown visitor, the neighbor and guest in the Bible? These are all "others." At all times and in all places people have dealt with others; they have accepted or rebuked, loved or hated, oppressed or liberated them. But we have become much more critically aware and reflective about our attitudes and treatment of others. We wrestle with the question of how to account for and deal with differences, whether religious, cultural, sexual or political. We can also rejoice in and celebrate the great diversity around us. We need significant others for our own development, for enriching relationships, but the otherness of others can also be deeply disconcerting and lead to rejection and exclusion.

It may come as a surprise to discover that Teilhard de Chardin also reflected on the significance of the other. Many years ago he expressed poignantly how in his own spiritual development the disturbing intrusion of the other was initially a problem:

> I find no difficulty in integrating into my inward life everything above and beneath me . . . in the universe—whether matter, plants, animals; and then powers, dominions and angels: . . . But "the other man" . . .—by which I do not mean "the poor, the halt, the lame and the sick," but "the other" quite simply as "other," the one who seems to exist independently of me because his universe seems closed to mine, and who seems to shatter the unity . . . of the world for me—would I be sincere if I did not confess that my instinctive reaction is to rebuff him? and that the mere thought of entering into spiritual communication with him disgusts me?[1]

This is an honest acknowledgment of an initial disposition that perhaps many share. It is not always easy to "love your neighbor," as the gospel commands. On the contrary, as Teilhard also knew, while it required not much effort to love those he was attracted to, he experienced an initial hostility to all others, to "the common run." He has described this shock of experiencing the other in *Le Milieu Divin*. I remember John Robinson feeling rather disconcerted about the above passage. He quoted it in his *Exploration into God*,[2] commenting that "even in the personalizing mysticism of Teilhard de Chardin there is the honest admission that 'other people' are much more like hell than heaven."[3] We all know that the experience of the other intruding into our world disrupts our complacency and closure. Teilhard expressed his difficulty in the form of a personal prayer:

> I confess, my God, that I have long been, and even now am, recalcitrant to the love of my neighbour. Just as much as I have derived intense joy in the superhuman delight of dissolving myself and losing myself in the souls for which I was destined by the mysterious affinities of human love, so I have always felt an inborn hostility to, and closed myself to, the common run of those whom You tell me to love . . .
>
> Grant, O God, that the light of Your countenance may shine for me in the life of that "other." The irresistible light of Your eyes shining in the depth of things has already guided me towards all the work I must accomplish, and all the difficulties I must pass through. Grant that I may see You, even and above all, in the souls of my brothers, at their most personal, and most true, and most distant.[4]

Otherness breaks the boundaries of our existence by disclosing new openings, leading to new questions, new horizons, possibly to infinity, to God. Teilhard realized that he was not drawn to the other simply through personal sympathy, but he was motivated to meet with and love the other through his love for God, through "the united affinities of a world for itself, and of that world for God."[5]

For the Christian, it is through the sacrament of the eucharist, through communion, that the other becomes spiritually especially significant. Teilhard addresses God about the other by saying:

> You do not ask for the psychologically impossible—since what I am asked to cherish in the vast and unknown crowd is never anything save one and the same personal being which is Yours.
>
> Nor do you call for any hypocritical protestations of love for my neighbour, because—since my heart cannot reach Your person except at the depths of all that is most individually and concretely personal in every "other"— it is to the "other" *himself*, and not to some vague entity around him, that my charity is addressed.[6]

In the same passage Teilhard describes how humanity is sleeping as long as it remains imprisoned "in the narrow joys of its little closed loves. A tremendous spiritual power is slumbering in the depths of our multitude, which will manifest itself only when we have learnt to *break down the barriers* of our egoisms and by a fundamental recasting of our outlook, raise ourselves up to the habitual and practical vision of universal realities."[7]

Amid the warring world of 1942 Teilhard wrote a thought-provoking, unpublished paper entitled "The Rise of the Other,"[8] in which he described this modern rise of the other as "the rise of number," "the rise of the collective," "the rise of the personal" and the "rise of sympathy with the other" or "the rise of the sense of man." For him this includes a sense of a shared venture, "the sense of an evolution in common,"[9] which is a new genesis. He described the ascent of all humans together metaphorically as a "voyage" on the sea. Speaking about his own experience he wrote, "Whenever the chances of life bring me into contact with another man whom, however alien he may be to me by nationality, class, race or religion, I find closer to me than a brother, *because he, too, has seen the ship and he, too, feels that we are steaming ahead,*" with both of them sharing the sense of a common destiny. There is the increasing pressure of numbers; there are growing bonds of collectivization; and there is "the irresistible rise of the other all around us" intruding into our individual lives.[10]

It is a reflection on the personal and collective interacting in the transformation of our world whose dynamic Teilhard perceived so clearly. But instead of seeing this process of "the rise of the other" as a threat, he sees it mainly as a tremendous possibility for greater union and communion.

For the Christian believer it is ultimately in communion with God that we can be truly in communion with others, that we can learn to respect and love their otherness in its own right, so that others become transformed from strangers and aliens into friends and neighbors. In Teilhard's view "the only human embrace capable of worthily enfolding the divine is that of all people opening their arms to call down and welcome the Fire. The only subject ultimately capable of mystical transfiguration is the whole group of humankind forming a single body and a single soul in charity."[11]

This is a truly mystical vision, a spiritual goal of unity and wholeness that requires the powers of faith, whether religious, humanistic or idealistic. In actual practice we are all too painfully aware of our brokenness and fragmentation, of oppression and exploitation setting diverse human groups against each other. In our postcolonial world we hear so many other voices—voices of people who were colonized and oppressed but who now speak in their own right, on behalf of themselves. There exist many groups of "others" in today's world. I will focus on the otherness represented by the peoples of the so-called Third World, now more often described as peoples from the South. Each of these terms has its own conceptual difficulties. It seems appropriate to speak of the Third World in connection with theology and spirituality because this expression is still widely used, especially by the Ecumenical Association of Third World Theologians (EATWOT), founded in 1976.

Seeking Christian renewal, what can we in the First World learn from the theology and spirituality of the Third World?

Third World Theology and Spirituality

It is in the Third World that Christianity is most clearly put to the test. It is here that Christianity is at its most diverse, its most creative, its most vibrant. Most Christians now live in the Third World, often in a minority situation, challenged by the otherness of surrounding religious and cultural differences. Historically, most of Christian theology has been produced in the West. Modern Reformation and post-Reformation theology was formulated in Europe, much of it in the categories of the enlightenment. It is this dominance of European thought forms in theological discourse that Third World theologians now call radically into question.

It is clear that within the larger social and historical context of Third World societies the same theological questions arise that Teilhard de Chardin asked from 1919 onward: What is the meaning of the gospel? What is essential and central to Christianity, and what is redundant? What is the new kind of theology we need for the new season and age we live in? What kind of spirituality can feed and sustain the struggle of life and lead us to God?

Third World theologians are doing theology within a new context. Their questions and answers are rooted in praxis. It is their practical experience combined with biblical and theological resources that leads them to new theological reflection. Their theology is thus rightly called a contextual theology, which methodologically and conceptually is very different from the overintellectual, even rationalistic habits of modern Western theology. Contextual theology requires personal engagement and commitment. Because of this, Third World theology is closely intertwined with questions of practical spirituality.

The Ecumenical Association of Third World Theologians brings together theologians from Asia, Africa and Latin America, but also from marginalized communities in societies of great wealth, whether blacks or Hispanics in the United States, the Palestinian Christians in Israel and the Middle East, or disinherited people in South Africa, Japan, New Zealand and Australia. The challenge of Third World theology to traditional ways of theological thinking was first clearly expressed at the fifth international EATWOT conference, held in 1981 in New Delhi in India.

The conference proceedings were published under the title *Irruption of the Third World: Challenge to Theology.*[12] As the editors explained, the term "Third World," first used in the sixties, had by the eighties acquired several layers of meaning. These varied "from the purely geographic ('the South') to the socio-economic ('poor') to the political ('non-aligned') and even the theological ('from the underside of history')." To those who met in Delhi, Third Worldness was characterized by massive poverty and oppression.[13]

The Delhi meeting was described as "the irruption of the Third World" onto the world theological scene, calling for vigorous theological transformation and renewal. It became clear that, however different in their local settings, all Third World theologies share certain commonalities in terms of their methodologies, their socioeconomic and political contexts, their encounter with non-Christian religions and cultures and their search for liberation from poverty and oppression, linked to a particular biblical hermeneutics. But there were specific challenges, too, that theologians from different continents had to face. For theologians from South America it was particularly the challenge of the class struggle, for Africans the challenge of the indigenization of Christianity within African culture and for Asians the challenge of religious pluralism and the great wisdom traditions of Asia that required new theological reflection and response.

I quote some passages from the final statement of the Delhi conference:

> Inasmuch as the vast majority of the Third World people are those of other faiths, the irruption of the Third World is an irruption of a world that is not Christian. It is bursting into history with a voice of its own, demanding justice and equality, reaffirming its age-old religions and cultures, and challenging the West-oriented and narrowly Christian understanding of the world and of history. No social revolution in the Third World can be effective or lasting unless it takes into account and incorporates the religious experience of the people . . .

> The tools and categories of traditional theology are inadequate for doing theology in context. They are still too wedded to Western culture and the capitalist system. Traditional theology has not involved itself in the real drama of a people's life, or spoken in the religious and

cultural idioms and expressions of the masses in a meaningful way. It has remained highly academic, speculative, and individualistic, without regard for the societal and structural aspects of sin . . .

A renewal of theology should bring about not only new articulations but a new spirituality deriving from the positive inspirations of our cultures and of our struggles.[14]

It was recognized that in this search for renewal different regions of the world give quite different emphases to the expression of spirituality. For example, many Christians in Central America "are reliving the exodus, the covenant, and the paschal mystery, and discovering the saving God in that experience,"[15] whereas Christians in India are experiencing new ways of seeing the Divine through traditional Indian religions. The spiritual significance and challenge of the otherness of different religions is well summed up by the Sri Lankan theologian Aloysius Pieris when he says that this encounter in the Third World "vivifies the Christian kerygma by recharging the three key words round which it revolves, words now worn out by ideological misuse: *basileia* (the new order), *metanoia* (interior conversion to that order), and *martyrion* (overt commitment to it)."[16]

Through interreligious encounter in a religiously plural society people discover the otherness of different spiritual traditions and religious world views. It is not surprising that several participants at the World Council of Churches "Spirituality in Interfaith Dialogue" in 1987 in Kyoto, Japan,[17] spoke from a perspective of having personally encountered religious diversity in the Third World, especially in Asia. Christians from the Roman Catholic, Protestant and Orthodox traditions asked themselves what dialogue with and sharing in the spiritualities of other faiths can contribute to the life of ordinary Christian individuals and communities:

What individual spiritual journeys have led Christians into the spiritual life of other religious traditions? What problems have they encountered in this pursuit, and what insights and perspectives have they gained?

What kinds of mutual enrichment have they found in

spiritual dialogue with people of other faiths? What have they discovered in the traditions of the other? What have they rediscovered in their own traditions?[18]

These questions were still more poignantly expressed during the Third General Assembly of EATWOT, held in 1992 in Nairobi, Kenya. Its overall theme was "Spirituality of the Third World: A Cry for Life."[19] As so often in Third World theology, the collective endeavor of reflecting together produced a moving and theologically challenging final statement, "A Cry for Life," from the many peoples around the world who suffer extremes of poverty and injustice. They draw on all their spiritual resources to carry on their struggle and resistance against the forces of oppression. I quote some passages from this document:

> The very word "spirit" is an acknowledgement that human life is propelled by a principle beyond human power and knowledge. Unable to define this sense of being touched by the beyond, the word spirituality has come to our aid as a convenient term to articulate the sense of our being moved by a spiritual energy to hold on to life and to live it to the fullest. Spirituality spells our connectedness to God, to our human roots, to the rest of nature, to one another and to ourselves. Our spirituality is our experience of the Holy Spirit moving us and our communities to be life-giving and life-affirming . . .
>
> We live our spirituality in creative response to the cry for life, the cry for God. We celebrate our spirituality in songs, rituals and symbols which show the energizing Spirit animating the community to move together in response to God. All existence is spiritual, our way of life as Third World peoples is spiritual. The spiritual traditions of the indigenous peoples—Native Americans, Aborigines, Maoris, Dalits, Tribal peoples of India and Black Africans in Africa—are a powerful reminder of this fact. The spirituality of these people recognizes the "personhood" of all things in creation and leads therefore to a deep respect for nature . . . There is a life force that urges them to seek the glory of God and of creation by

seeking the glory of the whole of humanity, for to do so is to seek a humanity fully alive . . .

There is no room for romanticizing spirituality. It is a cry for life, a power to resist death and the agents of death. Spirituality is the name we give to that which provides us with the strength to go on, for it is the assurance that God is in the struggle. Spirituality involves people's resistance to dehumanization and fulfills the quest for self-discovery, self-affirmation and self-inclusion, for in each of us in the whole human community is the urge to live and to live fully as human beings . . .

Our language about spirituality uses expressions such as "spirituality for liberation, spirituality for struggle, spirituality of involvement, spirituality of combat." The current use of spirituality is not one that directs us to the next world but to justice here and now. Spirituality is not a call away from life but the life force that urges us on to do justice and to resist evil. We are dealing here with Jesus' spirituality, one that is the source of justice and righteousness.[20]

This document expresses strongly how spirituality arises out of life and is interwoven with all its patterns and expressions, how it is in the midst of life that we experience and are led to God. Other parts of the same document deal with more traditional theological themes, with the role of the Bible and the Jesus of faith. Jesus is proclaimed the Lord, but "this does not mean that we need to impose him on everyone else. For though Jesus . . . truly puts us in touch with God, . . . the absolute mystery of Godhead cannot be wholly comprehended in Jesus. For God is beyond all name and form, and the many insights we have into God cannot singly or collectively exhaust the mystery of God's being."[21]

Christology, therefore, must not be an "imperial christology," such as was brought to the Third World

by a colonial Christianity which denied other religions (and other cultures) the right to exist, and claimed a monopoly for salvation. Jesus' own words are not the triumphalistic words of the imperialist Christ of the colonial Christianity, but words of love and service. He

comes so that we may have life and have it in abundance
... In our struggle for liberation we have discovered a
common commitment in people belonging to quite different faiths; and our religious life as Third World Christians is, in fact, lived out of two great traditions—both
the Christian tradition and the traditions of our indigenous religions.[22]

The efforts of Third World theologians to reclaim their traditions[23] and develop a life-affirming spirituality leading to full
humanity share a close affinity with many of the intentions
so deeply felt by Teilhard de Chardin, although Third World
theologians go far beyond him in developing the particular
details of their theology and spirituality. But there exists
among them, similar to Teilhard, the search for a greater unity
of humanity, the trust in and commitment to life, the attempt
to formulate a new, more integral and universal theology, the
emphasis on a vibrant, life-affirming spirituality so urgently
needed for the transformation of individuals and communities, the expressions of a new christology that in Asia is both
a new perception of the human Jesus and a newly expressed
theology of the cosmic Christ.

The "cry for life" is movingly expressed in a poem that pref-
aces the final statement of the 1992 EATWOT assembly.

> Cry, cry, cry for life
> For the living, for the dead
> For the desert, for the sea
> Poisoned fish, birds with broken wings
> Poets with no words
> Singers without a song.
> . . . .
> Cry, cry, cry for life
> For the courage, for the hope
> For the forest, for the stream
> Bodies may die, spirit never dies
> In our struggle, we burst in songs
> As a new day dawns, we will shout in joy.[24]

Among the numerous currents now challenging traditional
theology mentioned in the final conference statement, Third

World theologians list in first place women's struggle against violence and their cry for life,[25] but also women's own religious and spiritual resources. How do theology, spirituality and the voices of women come together in Third World theology?

Theology, Spirituality and the Voices of Women

Women have been the "other" par excellence in human history and culture. Sexually different and other from men, we women have been in the past defined by and dependent on men without a right to our own voice and to an independent role. Theologically, too, women have been assigned a position of inferiority and subjugation. It is only in the modern period that the biblical teaching about both man and woman being created in the image of God, each representing the *imago Dei,* has been interpreted in a truly egalitarian sense, affirming equality and partnership.[26] This biblical teaching was certainly of considerable importance in the emergence of the first phase of the women's movement in the mid-nineteenth century, and it is also much commented upon in contemporary feminist theology today.

Since women gained access to theological education—a process that also began in the mid-nineteenth century—and have become theologically literate, they have developed critical tools for the analysis of traditional theological teachings, so much rooted in a patriarchal and androcentric world view. Far from being just a Western development, feminist theology is situated and occurs in a global context today.[27] Christian women around the world are engaging in and doing theology in a new way. Whereas in the past there was a silence and invisibility of women in theology, there is now a new awakening of women in church life and theological thinking. Women are no longer simply objects of theology studied by men; they are subjects, practitioners and producers of theology.

Feminist theology has already fanned out into several specialized fields of study, but the term "feminist theology" is too restrictive for what is happening among Christian women around the whole world. The voices of women are heard in

public everywhere. This new awakening at a *global* level is a
true *novum* in human history and consciousness. Women are
doing theology; reflecting theologically on their experience;
struggling against oppression, exclusion and marginalization;
applying a hermeneutic of suspicion to traditional theological sources and teachings. In contrast with feminist theology,
the term "women's theology" is wider, more inclusive of many
women's activities within church communities. It can be applied more easily worldwide than the more specialized, more
academic term "feminist theology." All women's theology tries
to overcome the *theological apartheid* that has existed between men and women for most of Christian history. Thus it
is not surprising that some commentators today consider the
development of women's theology one of the most promising
and vibrant developments in contemporary Christianity,
closely linked to new experiments and understandings in spirituality.

Much more could be said about this, but I shall restrict my
remarks to the theology and spirituality voiced by women
from the Third World. It is here that particularly creative
and challenging developments occur.

If woman is the other, a Third World woman is doubly other.
This double repression is very clear from the struggle Third
World women theologians have had within the Ecumenical
Association of Third World Theologians itself. If the 1981 New
Delhi conference was characterized as the irruption of the
Third World into theology, the women's voices raised at that
conference have been movingly described by the African Mercy
Amba Oduyoye as "the irruption within the irruption."[28]

Third World women have a double struggle—they struggle
against the oppressive patriarchy of Third World men as well
as against what has been called the racism of the feminists of
the First World. The context and struggle of Third World
women highlight the interstructured nature of oppression:
Issues of sexism, race, class and colonialism are closely interwoven in women's experience. What is remarkable is the speed
and efficiency with which Third World women theologians
have networked with each other and organized themselves.

After the EATWOT meeting in New Delhi in 1981, the issue of sexism came fully to the fore at the next conference of

the Ecumenical Association of Third World Theologians, in Geneva in 1983. The women participants founded their own Women's Commission of EATWOT, which has since then organized regional, continental and intercontinental women's conferences on theology and spirituality. The last one was held in Costa Rica in 1994. It brought together women theologians from the South and the North, from the Third and the First Worlds, to dialogue with each other. These conferences of Third World women theologians are important milestones in the development of women's theology worldwide.[29]

The Third World women theologians work with each other and, at the same time, they also collaborate with the male theologians in EATWOT. In fact, women theologians soon represented more than a third of the EATWOT membership, a higher proportion than found in most Western theological societies and organizations. Much of women's theology in the Third World shares the same context as that of male Third World theologians, but it also has its own specific characteristics. Women are doing theology out of their own experience, and this experience is often different from that of their men folk. As the Korean woman theologian Chung Hyun Kyung has said, she wants to do theology in a way that her mother can understand. Women's experiences of poverty, oppression, violence and pain—what the Mexican theologian Elsa Tamez, now president of the Latin American Biblical Seminary in Costa Rica, has called "the power of the naked"[30]—provide much of the context of this.

After acquiring advanced theological education and traditional academic degrees, often obtained in the West, Third World women theologians are "seeing theology with new eyes." They apply their theological thinking to their own context, which leads them to develop new methods and insights. They are not interested in creating theological systems, a new systematic, constructive theology produced by an individual theological thinker who claims name and fame for it. Much of their theological work arises out of community, that of their different churches and that of networking with other women. Thus many statements are worked out collaboratively rather than by individuals working alone. The experience of participating and working in community seems to be more developed among these women than among most Western women theologians, who often tend to work in the same individualistic and competitive style as their male colleagues. Such a strong community context also affects the style and content of individual women writers. Women theologians in the Third World have developed a tremendous resilience and strength through new bonding. Their critique of oppression and inequality, and of an oppressive patriarchal theology, is truly radical and transformative. But it is not confrontational, for it remains in dialogue with others. Its character can be aptly summarized as "gentle but radical."[31]

Third World women's theology is above all a passionate commitment, an endeavor that is "the fruit of passion and compassion." This emotional and existential engagement was underwritten by the title the first intercontinental women's conference in Mexico in 1986 chose for its published proceedings: *With Passion and Compassion: Third World Women Doing Theology.*[32]

The Brazilian theologian María Clara Bingemer, one of five women professors at the Jesuit Faculty in Rio de Janeiro, expressed a similar idea more poignantly when she argued that the challenge of women doing theology is the "challenge to *restore the primacy of desire within theological discourse.*" In her article "Women in the Future of the Theology of Liberation" she wrote:

The future of the female way of doing theology is . . . inseparably linked with desire. The primacy of rationality must be replaced by the primacy of desire, the cold circumspection of purely scientific inquiry must give way to a new sort of systematics springing from the impulse of desire that dwells at the deepest level of human existence and combines sensitivity and rationality, gratuitousness and effectiveness, experience and reflection, desire and rigor. "God is love" (1 John 4:8). If this is so, God can only be, in the beginning, the object of desire; not of necessity, not of rationality. Theology—which seeks to be reflection and talk about God and God's word—therefore cannot but be moved and permeated throughout its whole extent by the flame of desire . . .

Born of desire, theology exists as theology only if it is upheld and supported by desire, in the direction of the desire that is its goal and its horizon.

The presence of women in the world of theology brings back to the front line, to the front of the stage of the church's life, that primacy of desire for which purely rational concepts do not allow. A woman finds it unthinkable to divide her own being into watertight compartments and treat theological work as a purely rational activity. Moved by desire . . . she does theology with her body, her heart and hands, as much as with her head . . .

In this way the Spirit, the motor and origin of desire, poured out on history and humanity, finds good and fertile ground for creative imagination . . . At the center of theological reflection and discourse, which remain open to a future still not fully explored, the Spirit reinstates the rights of the poetic and symbolic as literary genres, the only ones able to reach the heart of the matter and touch the hem of the Spirit and of Beauty.[33]

This is a strong statement, which I fully endorse, although I would argue that it is not only women who allow themselves "to be possessed by the desire that inflames and summons, that keeps alight, not consumes, the flame of love in the face of everything that threatens to extinguish it."[34] We find the flame of love and desire in many mystics, and it is certainly present in Teilhard de Chardin who, I think, would have been delighted with describing the theological challenge as one "to restore the primacy of desire within theological discourse."

Until recently theological reflection was almost exclusively undertaken by men. In María Clara Bingemer's view, shared by many other women doing theology around the globe, this one-sided, partial theology "has lacked the desire, the heart, the body, and the head of a woman to enable it to be more fully itself, to enable new treasures to be discovered and brought to birth out of the womb of God's word, so that the image of god—man and woman—could be more perfectly revealed and made known."[35]

The Korean Chung Hyun Kyung speaks of the "violence of abstraction" so characteristic of Western theology. She describes a new and very different understanding of theology arising out of the popular life and experience of the people. This theology is a cry, a plea, an invocation, a vision quest, an embodied, critical reflection that is not primarily "God-talk," but "God-praxis."[36] This is a spiritual task as much as a theological one.

New theological insights among women theologians from Africa, Asia, Latin America, from minority groups in North America and elsewhere, relate to new ways of approaching the Bible, new ways of reflecting on Jesus, Mary and the church, new ways of celebrating the eucharist and other sacraments, new ways of experiencing the living God "who is the center from which all theology emanates and on which it all converges."[37]

Central to and closely interwoven with all these developments is a newly emerging spirituality. There exists both an implicit and an explicit spiritual dimension in the contemporary women's movement as a whole.[38] In fact, the development of the women's movement, the liveliness and dynamic of its debate, the rich diversity of women's voices, can be read as signs of the spiritual creativity of our culture, as pointers to new horizons and new sources of transformative empowerment. In Latin America women's search for spirituality in the midst of poverty, oppression and injustice has also been described as a "cry for life, a new way of acting in the power of the Spirit.[39]

The Hispanic women in the United States who call themselves *mujeristas* coined the challenging expression *spirituality as a struggle for life*. This is rich with resonance, a vibrant, thought-provoking statement that invites unpacking. It is as simple as it is bold. For these women spirituality is not something that occurs only in a specifically religious context, set apart by sacred time and space, surrounded by institutional walls and mental categories of separation that make it a safe haven or distant island rarely visited and difficult to reach.

On the contrary, spirituality is a force of survival, a creative, inspiring power to struggle and resist; it is like daily food and sustenance in the struggle to overcome violence and oppression, to achieve transformation and wholeness. But women's spirituality is not only a struggle *for* life—to find more life and a better life, and find it abundantly—it is also a spirituality *of* life through which women are nourished by the process and energies of life itself, through new birth and further growth. Such a spirituality of and for life is continually strengthened and renewed through our experiences of work and struggle from which we can draw spiritual insight and new energy if we but learn how to be spiritually transformed by everything that comes *into* our life. I think this is what Teilhard de Chardin meant when he said "Always trust life" and when he described the whole of life as one single communion. Such spirituality grows further and deeper through prayer, silent contemplation and communion in worship and action. Such spirituality is the breath and blessing of life, the very bread and leaven of life that makes our individual, personal life with its sufferings, joys and pain rise anew and transforms it into something greater.

Christian women in Asia, perhaps more than anywhere else, live in the midst of a religiously plural world, especially rich in ancient wisdom traditions. Women are deeply challenged by the existence and witness of these different religious traditions, especially in their reflections on a newly emerging spirituality. Their new experiences and insights are sometimes stated collectively, or on occasion highlighted by individual women theologians. Chung Hyun Kyung argues in *Struggle to Be the Sun Again*[40] that, in encounter with the indigenous and wisdom traditions of Asia, Christian spirituality will move away from a "Christo-centrism" toward "life-centrism."[41] She pleads for a woman-affirming, body-loving and nature-honoring spirituality that is truly ecumenical as well as creation-centered. It is this radical openness that made her reflections and prayer to the Holy Spirit so controversial at the 1991 WCC Assembly in Canberra.[42]

The Philippine Sister Mary John Mananzan describes the newly emerging spirituality among Asian women as a continuing process that is self-affirming, empowering, integral rather than dualistic, liberating, contemplative and healing. It is not a Good Friday spirituality, but an easterly spirituality that feasts more than it fasts, that prefers celebration to asceticism, for "you cannot have a revolution without a guitar."[43]

This is a spirituality that truly liberates the spirit; it is spirituality as a *necessity* rather than a luxury, the promise of fullness and freedom, of wholeness and redemption for all humankind and all creation. Such an understanding of spirituality is close to many ecotheological concerns, for it is a spirituality that is cosmically rooted in all of life and ultimately embraces the whole of the earth. Thus it is marked by interconnectedness at all levels, so that reality is experienced as an immense web rather than a hierarchical pyramid of being. It is particularly this feature of interconnectedness, of the organic continuity of life at all levels, that the new spirituality of women shares with the holistic, integral thinking of Teilhard de Chardin, who praised the powers of the earth and the beauty of life, sang a hymn to the universe and celebrated the spiritual power of matter.[44]

Such a spirituality is lively and vigorous; it is a spirituality for struggle and involvement, but also for liberation and transformation. In such a spirituality the threads of immanence and transcendence are intertwined anew to form a stronger, more inclusive pattern. For a person of Christian faith a renewed and vibrant spirituality provides a powerful attraction to see all things in Christ and Christ in all things from a fresh and very different perspective than in the past. How such a perspective can lead to a spirit of renewal and transformation for our planet will be explored in the next chapter.

Such transformation requires that spirituality is no longer considered a luxury for a few, for an educated elite and leisured class, for religious specialists and believers. At this point in history spirituality is a necessity for all if we want to create a world of peace and justice while safeguarding the integrity of creation. As mentioned in an earlier chapter, we have to be attentive to spiritual issues in education, not just in religious education but in all educational contexts wherever they are. It is perhaps less important to define exactly *what spirituality is* than *what it does*—to us, to our communities, to our environment. In listening to the voices around the world—whether the voices of women, the voices from the Third World or the voices of spiritual seekers from different religious traditions—we have to learn to respond to multiple otherness. We must take responsibility *for the other* and *for each other* in mutuality. Understanding spirituality in such an all-embracing, comprehensive sense brings into play personal, political and global concerns. It is these that I shall address next.

CHAPTER EIGHT

Christian Spirituality

*Seeds for the Renewal and Transformation
of Our Planet*

ᗰᙡᙢᎧ

Each year we experience the beautiful, promising days of
spring. We sense the joy of new life, we feel the freshness of
color and light, the exuberant new growth in gardens and
fields. There is the wonder of a new greening of the earth, a
bursting forth of flowers and blooms, a new energy that draws
us upward to horizons of hope and renewal. The cyclical pattern of the seasons, the new growth of plants, the birth of the
young, have always given people hope and new energy. The
renewal of spring always encourages faith and hope. Its annual occurrence is a clear proof of the possibilities of a new
beginning, the emergence of a new zest that encourages us to
renew our own powers, to think afresh and act anew. The
possibilities of new birth, of a new beginning in the natural
world, give us strong grounds for hope that renewal is possible in our social world, too, that we can draw on new energies, envisage the world anew and strengthen our will to make
our dream of a better world and a more humane society come
true.

Thinking of new birth and growth, how can we renew and
strengthen our Christian faith?

The Jesuit scientist and mystic Pierre Teilhard de Chardin
was deeply aware of the urgent need for Christian renewal,
as I have shown throughout this book. As early as 1926 he
wrote to one of his friends, the Abbé Christophe Gaudefroy:

"It sometimes seems to me that there are three perishable stones sitting dangerously in the foundations of the present Church: the first is a government which excludes democracy; the second is a priesthood which excludes and minimizes women; the third is a revelation which excludes prophecy for the future."[1]

This was said with reference to the Roman Catholic church. Seen from a contemporary perspective, it is an amazingly insightful remark. It points clearly to some of the greatest problems in modern Roman Catholicism with its hierarchical structures, its exclusion of women, and its condemnation of different prophetic voices within its own midst. Teilhard himself can be seen as such a prophetic voice silenced by the church during his lifetime and marginalized since his death—so much so that his inspiring example and reflections on Christian renewal are seldom mentioned by those who have Christian spirituality at heart.

Misunderstandings and Controversies about Teilhard's Thought

For example, it is sad to learn that a great and influential spiritual writer like Thomas Merton did not know Teilhard's writings, nor did he want to know them because his work had been censured. In September 1966 Merton wrote to the young theologian Rosemary Ruether: "I haven't really read much Teilhard since an article of mine on the *Divine Milieu* was not allowed to be published by the Censors of the Order (Teilhard too wicked). I was not sufficiently concerned to read him when I couldn't do anything with it—I am not sold enough on him to read it for pure illumination and uplift. So I didn't read him."[2]

This passage raises the question about the general reception of Teilhard's thought by other Christians, or rather the uninformed rejection of it by different Catholics. In the late 1960s, in one of her early letters to Thomas Merton, Rosemary Ruether associated Teilhard with the Catholic Hegelians. As a Christian activist working for social justice she thought that Teilhard had "no sense of radical evil and, so ultimately, becomes rather inhuman."[3] This is another assessment by a leading Catholic writer based on insufficient knowledge of Teilhard's work. To be fair, Ruether has drawn more extensively and positively on Teilhard's thought in her more recent book, *Gaia and God,* about which more later.

An early example of Catholic censorship of Teilhard's ideas is provided by an incident told in Julian Huxley's *Memories,* written in the early seventies. When Julian Huxley was Director of UNESCO in Paris, he met Teilhard on several occasions and was much taken by him. He admired him greatly and felt they both were "in almost general agreement over the essential facts of cultural and organic evolution," although Huxley did not share Teilhard's religious beliefs and acknowledged their "ineradicable divergence of approach." After Teilhard's death Huxley agreed to write the preface to the English edition of *The Phenomenon of Man* and was bitterly attacked by some of his rationalist friends "for supporting a religious (and not fully scientific) work!"[4]

The incident, which Huxley reports at some length, occurred in 1955, shortly after Teilhard's death. The French Catholic University in Montreal, Canada, organized a public event, chaired by the vice-chancellor and announced as an "unbiased enquiry" into the theological and scientific aspects of Teilhard's work. Huxley and his wife were among the packed audience in the Magna Aula of the university and Huxley's *Memories* includes the following description of what happened:

> The rostrum was occupied by a long table at which were sitting five lay professors and several clerical theologians, including a grim and majestic Dominican Abbé in beautiful white robes . . .
>
> One by one, the theologians and the professors got up and said their piece. Was Père Teilhard a good scientist? No, he was not. Was he a competent philosopher? No, he was not. Was he a sound methodologist? No, he was not. People call him a geologist, but he was only an amateur. People call him a theologian—but was he? Finally, the Dominican rose to sum up. He spoke in beautiful French and went through all the arguments. The audience sat spellbound. The Abbé in his sculptural white robes

studied all the faces turned towards him, awaiting his verdict. He raised his hand from the ample folds of his cassock: Père Teilhard, he said, was a poet. "Ses paroles somptueuses sont un piège. Prenez garde de ne pas y tomber." He sat down in profound silence. Teilhard and all his works had been condemned.[5]

This report is an extraordinary testimony to the fact that in spite of almost all his religious works still being unpublished in 1955, Teilhard's name and ideas were sufficiently well known among a French-speaking public to attract wide public attention, but also cause fear and a defensive attitude among traditional Roman Catholics.

It is interesting how Huxley reacted to this experience, especially when he was invited by the vice-chancellor to speak because he had known Teilhard personally. His account continues:

> I accepted, and walked up to the rostrum. Turning to face the audience, I explained that, from my personal knowledge, Père Teilhard was a completely sincere man, an excellent paleontologist, and that although I did not agree with him on all points, I considered that his reconciliation of scientific fact and religious belief along evolutionary lines was enlightened and helpful. There was a burst of spontaneous applause from the audience, as of great tension released. The clapping continued for several minutes, while the panel of assessors looked glum. As I went out of the hall, happy to have done something to vindicate my old friend, I was besieged by eager young questioners.[6]

Is this occurrence perhaps indicative of a larger trend whereby Teilhard will be better understood and more appropriately acknowledged by nonbelievers than by Christians? Huxley also mentions how "Teilhard has posthumously become a prophet, indeed almost a saint, in France, as well as in many other countries." He sees his writings as "a symbol of the reconciliation between scientific humanism and Catholic orthodoxy, which the younger generation of religiously-minded people, including many Catholics, ardently desired." Yet when writing this in 1973 he also felt that some papal utterances and encyclicals had set back the hopes for such reconciliation in the near future.[7]

Teilhard has much to offer for Christian renewal, but also for a more coherent, more balanced relationship between science and religion, where his work is equally underrepresented in contemporary discussions.

For Teilhard a strongly life-affirming Christian renewal cannot happen without a new, more holistic attitude to the universe, to the world around us and to ourselves. For him spiritual renewal is centered on the cosmic Christ, which he understands as the Christ-element in all things and the presence of Christ throughout the entire cosmos. "Seeing Christ in all things" is a truly cosmo-theandric vision, which Teilhard expressed in a new way by bringing together the deepest insights of modern science and those of an ecological consciousness with an all-encompassing spiritual and deeply mystical vision.

When Chung Hyun Kyung affirms, as mentioned in the previous chapter, that Christian spirituality must move away from "Christo-centrism" toward a "life-centrism," this can sound like two mutually exclusive positions. But this is misleading, for these two are not real alternatives. So to divide Christ from life is a false dichotomy, for it is precisely in Christ, the cosmic Christ in whom all things move and have their being, that we find the fullness and center of all life as understood today, with all the diverse layers and complexities that our multiple life-worlds encompass. At present, these worlds long for deep transformation and renewal.

Our Planet and the Need for Transformation

People all over the world dream of a world different from the one we live in. They hope, work and pray for a better world, a more just and peaceful world freed from wars and tensions. To transform our planet from one of dissension and disorder, from war, violence and strife, into one of peace and harmony and to prevent ecological disaster does mean a change of heads and hearts. At present we have a world more torn apart than ever before in human history.[8] Yet it is also a world that longs to be one.

To change our world means that we have to foster the resolve and develop the commitment and will to change our ways. Only then can we create a new global order animated by a different, a new spirit. This will not be possible without a spiritual renewal and a return to the values of life, and a common commitment to a qualitatively better life for all. Religious and spiritual renewal now occur in a secular, pluralistic context, and religions must relate and speak to that context. Both the study of different religions and interreligious encounter can help us to foster a new spirit among different believers so that religions can learn to foster peace rather than violence and dissension around the globe. But for this to happen, renewal and reform have to take place within each of the different religions themselves.

Much has been said and written on Christian reform and renewal. The suggestions are as numerous as they are contradictory. Yet however different the voices of reform are, it seems clear that a thorough renewal of the structures of the Christian churches is needed. What is even more urgently needed is a newly affirmed and clearly articulated Christian spirituality, one that is truly incarnate. Only then can Christian spirituality provide a leaven of transformation for our world. In contemporary terms this also means we need an *ecological* spirituality that links us in a new way to the whole of creation and gives us spiritual harmony and balance.

The previous chapters have dealt with several themes that are marked by strong ecological concerns. Embracing the whole of the earth, seeking the wholeness of the human community, working for a more balanced life of peace and justice, of harmony with nature, the emergence of a new awareness of the universe and our responsibility for the future well-being of planet earth—these are perspectives that run like threads through the debates of interfaith dialogue, the discussions of First and Third World theologians, of women theologians around the world. They are also central to the World Council of Churches' study on Justice, Peace and the Integrity of Creation (JPIC) and find an echo in the works of many contemporary commentators and writers. Such themes have strong resonances in Teilhard de Chardin's own work, in his concern for the earth, the place of the human being within nature, our responsibility for the future, and for the social and spiritual development of the human community.

Critical ecological voices began to be raised toward the end of Teilhard's life, but ecological awareness has greatly increased since then. Based on detailed studies and abundant data on the natural environment, ecological consciousness has become much more articulate. Our sense of the possibility of impending ecological disasters is much more acute than it was during Teilhard's lifetime. We now feel a great sense of urgency and are aware of an ethical imperative to develop more responsible attitudes and action toward the earth and its resources. Several different religions have produced studies on their attitudes to the environment and have published public declarations about responsible attitudes toward nature.

The first section of the *Declaration Toward a Global Ethic* produced by the Parliament of the World's Religions in 1993 deals with our urgent need for a culture of nonviolence and respect for life. It speaks of the infinite preciousness of human beings, but also of the protection, preservation, and care the lives of animals and plants deserve:

Limitless exploitation of the natural foundations of life, ruthless destruction of the biosphere, and militarization of the cosmos are all outrages. As human beings we have a special responsibility—especially with a view to future generations—for Earth and the cosmos, for the air, water, and soil. We are *all intertwined together* in this cosmos and we are all dependent on each other. Each one of us depends on the welfare of all. Therefore the dominance of humanity over nature and the cosmos must not be encouraged. Instead we must cultivate living in harmony with nature and the cosmos.[9]

To some, this may not be a strong enough expression of the change of heart and urgent action needed to bring about the necessary transformation in our attitudes to the environment. As is the case with any declaration, the demands are too vague and not sufficiently specific to be of much help. The ecological crisis must be spelled out in considerable detail to shock people into greater awareness and influence their will to change their habits.

The need to promote a radical agenda for positive change is strongly argued by the report of the Independent Commission on Population and Quality of Life, *Caring for the Future: Making the Next Decades Provide a Life Worth Living*.[10] It makes the important point that the "carrying capacity" of our planet is strictly limited while the "caring capacity" of humanity has no limits. But at present the human community lacks the political will to act at a global level and take care of "the global commons," such as water and oceans, the atmosphere and forests, for the good of all. The commission "believes that we must transcend a narrow focus on the material basis of survival. We need now to establish our psychological, spiritual, and political capacities to care for each other as a determinant of progress and survival. The ethic of care— defining us as human beings—surmounts economic rationale: it can counteract individualism and greed. Caring for ourselves, for each other, for the environment is the basis upon which to erect sustainable improvement of the quality of life all around us. The care ethic now requires a drastic shift in paradigm." The report seeks "a new humanism" in the context of dignity and care: "The notion of care for ourselves, for each other, and for the environment we occupy is the very basis on which the sustainable improvement of the quality of life must be developed."[11]

Caring for the Future is a good example of how a fresh vision about our planet, about population, education, health care, women, work and politics, can mobilize new resources and new social forces. Fresh thinking occurs in many areas, for example with regard to the understanding of pollution and development. It may be helpful to reflect briefly on the four kinds of pollution that, according to the Indian theologian Samuel Rayan, are a threat to life on earth and to the planet itself. Rayan speaks of physical, social, cultural and spiritual pollution, extending the meaning of the world "pollution" beyond its customary boundaries.[12]

Physical pollution is the most obvious and best known, for it is linked to the poisoning of earth, air and water, and of the living things that depend on them. Such contamination occurs through numerous chemicals produced by industry, nuclear technology and military activity, all of which are environmentally dangerous and destructive as well as very costly in financial resources.

Rayan speaks of *social pollution* as an ecological problem created by the existence of massive poverty and destitution with their degrading consequences, side by side with enormous wealth and affluence. This unequal relationship exists *within* different countries and even more *between* different countries of the world. The so-called developed countries have only "26 % of the world's population but consume 80 % plus of the world's paper, metals and commercial energy, eat fully half of the world's food and feed a quarter of the world's grain to their animals."[13]

Cultural pollution is described as "large-scale illiteracy, which is but one of the manifestations of the neglect of the masses by the elite; by colonial and elitist devaluation of people's cultures, experiences, achievements, and wisdom; and the consequent alienation from the people, their needs and potentialities, of the colonially educated few who are now at the helm of affairs."[14] This is related to cultural and economic dependence and neocolonial relationships between the Third World and the First.

Spiritual and moral pollution is linked to "greed, competition, and consumerism," the shortsightedness that goes for immediate gain and overuses scarce resources, the voracious acquisitiveness and the dehumanizing effect that the reign of quantitative measurement and market commodities has on people's lives.[15] Much more could be said here, but it is clear that the different kinds of pollution are interconnected and that true "development" of the earth and its peoples must include the idea of spiritual development for all. Such development is also an issue of fundamental justice and balance for the human community.

The transformation of our relationship to the earth has two different aspects. On the one hand we need to develop a greater spirit of caring for the earth; on the other hand, this spirit cannot develop in full without a change in our awareness of our connection with and dependence on the earth and its products. Today the religious spirit is drawing great strength from this discovery of our rootedness in the earth and the awakening of a new sense of the cosmic. Many Christians feel inspired by a new approach to the whole of creation and reappropriate a powerful *creation spirituality,* which has numerous antecedents in the Christian tradition.

These new developments are of immense importance for the future of humanity and planet earth. They also have a deep impact on all forms of contemporary spirituality and have led to the emergence of a new ecological spirituality—an ability to respond with integrity and profound concern to our critical ecological situation—affecting all faiths. But current ecological concerns are also bringing about the revival of very different ancient religious beliefs and practices, and the growth of new religious movements. There is talk about a new *ecotheology,* an *ecospirituality* that is more bound up with the development of the earth in the light of contemporary ecological concerns than is the case with creation spirituality.[16] There exist quite a few attempts to develop a stronger ecological spirituality, not least in ecofeminism where the concerns of the women's movement come together with those of the ecological movement in order to work out what in a recent book has been called *Women Healing Earth.*[17]

These are all new developments that re-vision spirituality ecologically. But what are the main concerns of the new ecological spirituality, especially among Christians?

Ecological Spirituality

Thomas Berry, the great contemporary Catholic thinker on ecology, has pointed out again and again how church authorities and many Christians show an amazing insensitivity to ecological issues. Yet these issues are the most urgent of all confronting humanity today. The "mutual enhancement of the human and natural" is a task Christians must dedicate themselves to, for in Berry's view, "the renewal of religion in the future will depend on our appreciation of the natural world as the locus for the meeting of the divine and the human. The universe itself is the primary divine revelation. The splendor and the beauty of the natural world in all its variety must be preserved if any worthy idea of the divine is to survive in the human community."[18] To renew the earth as "a bio-spiritual planet" we need to draw creatively on all our available spiritual disciplines, use all our educational resources and energies in efforts that cross the traditional boundaries between different religions, spiritualities and cultures.

Thinking of ecological spirituality also means that spirituality is understood in an evolutionary sense. Spirituality itself develops and unfolds so as to articulate the human condition in a way that is commensurate with a particular time and age. Contrary to an earlier instrumental attitude which explored and exploited nature, the ecological attitude approaches the natural world as our home and as a sanctuary that must be treated with responsibility, care and reverence.

In his article "Ecological Spirituality and Its Practical Consequences," the philosopher Henryk Skolimoski speaks about the need for "spiritual reconstruction," which is based on a reverential treatment of the world and ourselves.[19] According to him, "the true work of ecology is not only through campaigns to save this or that threatened habitat (though this is important too) but also creating an attitude of mind within which the ecological and spiritual are one."[20] From an ecological perspective "spirituality is not about what gods you praise and how piously you do it, but about how your life affects other human beings, and other beings in the universe, including natural habitats and Mother Earth herself."[21]

Nowhere has the theme of "mother earth," of sacred matter as sacred mother, been more explored than in contemporary ecofeminism, whether in Carol Adams's edited work *Ecofeminism and the Sacred*[22] or Eleanor Rae's *Women, the Earth, the Divine*[23] or many other publications that describe the earth as Gaia. Some connect this theme with the Mother Goddess; others understand it in a pantheistic or panentheistic sense. Apart from a general understanding of the universe as a self-regulating organism and a general emphasis on respect and care, for the reverence of life as sacred, and the need for "earth healing" to redeem and reverse our destruction and domination of the earth,[24] there seems no common doctrinal core to the various attempts to formulate a truly ecological spirituality. As always in newly emerging fields, much more reflective work and critical debate are needed for a clarification of all the issues involved.

This also applies to the attempts of developing a "Theology in Green" or foster the "greening" of the churches. If it were that simple, we could advance more quickly. It is not just a matter of incorporating some ecological concerns here and there, but of transforming our whole world view, our attitudes, our relationships, our ethics, our politics, our spirituality. The interconnectedness between the transformation of our world view and our social, political and economic actions is highlighted in Allerd Stikker's fine study *The Transformation Factor: Towards an Ecological Consciousness,*[25] which is deeply influenced by Teilhard's thought, linking it to new ideas among scientists, environmentalists, psychologists and futurologists. Many of Teilhard's ideas have practical and policy implications, fostering at the same time a more integral, more ecologically rooted spirituality that encourages us to embrace the earth and rediscover its precious sacredness. His work still has a great deal to give, as long as his ideas are critically appropriated rather than merely imitated and reiterated.

Teilhard's passionate commitment to God and the earth was expressed in one of his early prayers:

O God, I wish from now on
to be the first to become conscious
of all that the world loves, pursues, and suffers;

I want to be the first to seek,
to sympathize and suffer;
the first to unfold and sacrifice myself

to become more widely human
and more nobly of the earth
than any of the world's servants.[26]

Ecological Perspectives in Teilhard de Chardin

Teilhard's consciousness of the immensity of the earth and its people, their common origin and destiny, came fully into its own after he had traveled extensively and worked for quite

a few years in China. It was then that he began to write about
the "spirit of the earth" and of "building the earth."[27] During
his reflections in the trenches of the First World War the whole
world had already appeared to him as one great "thing," as if
perceived from the moon. He then described the globe as surrounded by a layer of blueness, which for him symbolized the
density of thought, the *noosphere* as a layer of mind within
the layer of life covering the earth. Many years later the image of our globe floating against a blue background became
familiar all over the world through the famous photograph
taken of the earth from the moon—the picture of our bluish-
green planet suspended in space and surrounded by black-
ness.

As Bernice Marie-Daly has pointed out:

> For . . . decades, we humans have viewed this marvelous
> sight, and it has impacted our psyches with deep images
> of interconnectedness and beauty. This picture has be-
> come for many of us a mandala of spiritual renewal and
> hope, an image of our evolution toward oneness and
> global awareness that Teilhard foresaw . . . However, for
> all its beauty, stillness, and simplicity, this earth por-
> trait does not convey the existence of the particulars: the
> varied racial, ethnic, religious, economic, and cultural
> diversities among humans, as well as the variety and
> splendor of myriad species of our planet.[28]

The current holism of environmental philosophy often risks
obliterating the uniqueness and importance of the individual
and the particular. It is therefore important to realize that
"our deep, holistic awareness of the interconnectedness of all
life must be *lived* awareness that we experience in relation to
particular beings as well as the larger whole."[29] Some of this
mutual interconnectedness was expressed in Teilhard's theory
of creative union, about which I spoke in an earlier chapter.
This theory maintains that through union with others the
particularity of the individual person and group is enhanced
and further differentiated, and thus creative union brings
about something new through forming a larger whole.

Almost a decade after completing *The Phenomenon of Man*
Teilhard provided a summary of his ecological vision of the

close interdependence of the *natural* and *human worlds* in his book *Man's Place in Nature*. Subtitled "The Human Zoological Group," this book is based on a series of lectures given at the Sorbonne during February-March 1949. For the description of the integral link between the *natural, human* and *divine* we have to look elsewhere, namely to his religious and mystical writings, such as *The Mass on the World* and the *Milieu Divin*.

The experiential, scientific starting point for Teilhard's views was the concrete contact with the earth and its surface, its rocks and stones, its soil, plants and animals, and the long history of their life. It was the study of geology and biology as well as his innate affinity for the beauty of nature that made him embrace the earth. For Teilhard the geologist, the Christian mystic and thinker so deeply shaped by the organic thought patterns of the modern life sciences, the study of geology truly revealed the "face of the earth" whose mountains, continents and oceans showed him *one* earth enveloped by layers of life and thought. This unified earth immersed in the immense process of life is linked to the building of a spiritual reality as vast as the earth. The evolutionary ascent of the increasing complexity of matter and life is seen by him as also a moral and spiritual ascent, a moving forward to the unification of consciousness and the building of a unified humanity journeying toward God, whose divine presence shines through all levels of the natural and the human.

In studying "man's place in nature" Teilhard discovered the unity between the earth and humankind, a humanity that is being drawn ever more closely together but is still searching for a center, a heart. As he wrote in *The Vision of the Past*:

> Around the sphere of the earth's rock-mass there stretches a real layer of animated matter, the layer of living creatures and human beings, the biosphere. The great educative value of geology consists in the fact that by disclosing to us an earth which is truly *one,* an earth which is in fact but a single body since it has a face, it recalls to us the possibilities of establishing higher and higher degrees of organic unity in the zone of thought which envelops the world. In truth it is impossible to keep one's gaze constantly fixed on the vast horizons

opened out to us by science without feeling the stirrings of an obscure desire to see people drawn closer and closer together by an ever-increasing knowledge and sympathy until finally, in obedience to some divine attraction, there remains but one heart and one soul on the face of the earth.[30]

In another passage he relates our understanding of a structurally convergent universe to our faith in God:

In such a system (a structurally convergent universe) it is impossible to love one's neighbour without drawing closer to God—and *vice versa* for that matter. This we know well enough. But it is also impossible—and this is less familiar to us—to love either God or our neighbour without being obliged to help in the progress of the earthly synthesis of spirit in its physical totality . . . because we love, and in order to love more—we find ourselves . . . sharing—we more and better than anyone—in all the struggles, all the anxieties, all the aspirations, and also all the affections, of the earth *in so far as all these contain within them a principle of ascension and synthesis.*[31]

But the success of such a synthesis is by no means assured. When passages such as the one just quoted are read out of context, Teilhard de Chardin is often misjudged as too optimistic a thinker. Yet he himself questioned whether the experiment we are part of might in fact be successful, whether it might lead to the unity we need. "*Synthesis implies risk*," he wrote. "Life is less certain than death."[32] If the pressure of the earth forces us into some form of coming together, it is not at all certain that "ultra-hominization" will occur. Certain external and internal conditions have to be met for human and natural life to remain in balance, and these conditions are a tremendous challenge to the human community. Life on earth will fail if the following external conditions are not met:

Should the planet become uninhabitable before mankind has reached maturity; should there be a premature lack of bread or essential metals; or, what would be still more serious, an insufficiency, either in quantity or quality, of cerebral matter needed to store, transmit, and increase the sum total of knowledge and aspirations that at any given moment make up the collective germ of the noosphere: should any of these conditions occur, then, there can be no doubt that it would mean the failure of life on earth; and the world's effort fully to center upon itself could only be attempted again elsewhere at some other point in the heavens.[33]

As to the internal conditions needed, these are bound up with the full exercise of human freedom: "a *know-how to do*" to avoid various traps and blind alleys such as "politico-social mechanization, administrative bottle-necks, over-population, counter-selections" and, most important "a *will to do*," not to opt out, not to be discouraged by difficulties or fears.[34]

From his perspective of almost fifty years ago Teilhard probably misjudged the continued availability of material and physical energy resources. The threat of diminishing material resources seemed to him less great than the internal perils that life faces from human freedom and "undisciplined emancipation." These, he felt, were "much more menacing." Yet he remained hopeful when he said that

> a living system . . . tends to correct and stabilise its progress to the extent that the two-fold faculty of foresight and choice arises within its elements at the same time as a sharper awareness of the end to be attained. If you have ten experts tackling the same task, there is less danger of their becoming disheartened and going astray in their work than if you have only one. This means that the more the noosphere convolutes upon itself, the greater are its chances of finally centering on itself . . .
>
> Nothing . . . can prevent man-the-species from growing still greater . . . so long as he preserves in his heart the passion for growth.[35]

And for Teilhard this means growth toward a central meeting point of the human and the Divine in the universe. He describes this as "the self-subsistent center and absolutely final principle of irreversibility and personalization: the one and only true Omega,"[36] which is for him the cosmic Christ, the face and heart of God in our world.

Spirit of Christ as Spirit of Renewal

"Seeing Christ in all things" means that there is a center, a heart, a divine element in everything there is, in everything that comes into being and grows into greater fullness of being, in all our experiences and in all things surrounding us. For Teilhard affirming Christ means affirming the fullness of life. This is a christology not primarily centered on the human Jesus, but on a Christ of cosmic proportions, a Christ walking many different roads and found in many different places. The complexity of things is such today that we are aware of far greater subtleness and differentiation with which to see "Christ in all things" than were Christians in the past.

For the Christian, the mutual co-inherence of all things comes together within the life of Christ, a life that breathes through all of creation, through the entire world. It is a life that pulsates through all things as the vivifying, strengthening Spirit. This divine Spirit can be understood as the most intimate, the most powerful, the most personal element that Teilhard, in analogy with the center of the human body, calls the "heart" of the world. It is Teilhard's immense trust in life and his love of the heart of Christ, the heart of God, that are at the center of his efforts toward the renewal of Christian spirituality.

For many people this may seem too anthropomorphic, too particularistic, too narrow. Why call the center and body of the world the figure and face, the heart of Christ? Why indeed? Buddhists will always speak of the Buddha-nature and the cosmic body of the Buddha; Hindus worship the cosmic figure of Vishnu, the *vishvarupa,* or the figure of Krishna as he reveals himself to his devotee Arjuna in the *Bhagavad Gita*. Little did Teilhard know of these striking parallels, just as he did not know of the tremendous cosmic vision we rediscover in Hildegard of Bingen, for example.

The specificity of all these different visions relates always to a particular religious tradition and a particular way of conceptualizing the Ultimate. These visions are not identical. Rather, they are alternatives, though not exclusively so, because they also share certain commonalities and point beyond themselves to a Reality we cannot grasp. In this sense different visions of faith are like different human languages—they all contain words and world views, but they conceptualize them very differently for human communication. Religion is the language of the human spirit, as are art and music and other expressions of human creativity that draw us out of ourselves into something greater and more powerful, a *dynamis* or force that provides the deepest energy and source for life. It can also provide us with the urgently needed spiritual resources to heal our world.

Rosemary Ruether, in *Gaia and God,* which bears the subtitle "An Ecofeminist Theology of Earth Healing," explores different resources of the Jewish and Christian traditions that may be of help to us in shaping new attitudes toward the earth.[37] One of these is the sacramental tradition, which sees the whole of creation as holy, as a path and pointer to God. Ruether's critical discussion of contemporary ecological theology deals with Matthew Fox's creation spirituality and Teilhard de Chardin's spirituality as two examples of this sacramental tradition. She writes: "Teilhard's thought would mesh well with the Gaia hypothesis, for he sees the planet earth as a living organism. Earth is one living organism, not only spatially, but across time."[38] But Teilhard's understanding of the evolutionary process as a complexification of matter implies a moral and spiritual ascent, a unification of consciousness and convergence in what he calls the Omega Point. Ruether interprets this as "the evolution of immanent deity or the cosmic Christ,"[39] but I think this is too simple and perhaps a reductionist way of interpreting Teilhard's understanding of Christ. Although Christ is involved in the entire process of the universe and the world-in-becoming, he is not a merely immanent deity but is also seen as transcendent to the entire process of creation. As Teilhard wrote in his first essay "The Cosmic Life":

God, who cannot in any way blend or be mingled with the creation which he sustains and animates and binds together, is none the less present in the birth, the growth and the consummation of all things.

The earthly undertaking which is beyond all parallel is the physical incorporation of the faithful into Christ and therefore into God. And this supreme work is carried out with the *exactitude and the harmony of a natural process of evolution.*

At the inception of the undertaking there had to be a transcendent act which in accordance with mysterious but physically regulated conditions, should graft the person of God into the human cosmos. This was the Incarnation . . .

The Incarnation means the renewal, the restoration, of all the energies and powers of the universe; Christ is the instrument, the Center and the End of all creation, animate *and* material; through him everything is created, hallowed, quickened. This is the constant, *general* teaching of St. John and St. Paul (that most "cosmic" of sacred writers), a teaching which has passed into the most solemn phrases of the liturgy, but which we repeat and which future generations will go on repeating to the end without ever being able to master or to measure its profound and mysterious meaning, bound up as it is with the comprehension of the universe.[40]

Sally McFague, in *The Body of God: An Ecological Theology,*[41] discusses the organic models of the relationship between God and the world. She points out that while traditional Christian thinking has been highly ambivalent toward an organic model of the world—because of its emphasis on a transcendent deity distinct from the world—exciting new possibilities for a reconsideration of this model are given by both process theology and the work of Teilhard de Chardin.[42] She also mentions his thought as part of the long tradition of Christian sacramentalism, which she, like Rosemary Ruether, stresses as a most valuable resource for contemporary ecological thinking. Christian sacramentalism

is the major way Christianity has preserved and developed an appreciation for nature. It has encouraged Christians to look upon the world as valuable—indeed,

as holy . . . Christian sacramentalism has included nature as a concern of God and a way to God rather than
limiting divine activity to human history. For these and
other reasons Christian sacramentalism should be encouraged. It is a distinctive contribution of Christianity.
From its incarnational base, it claims that in analogy
with the body of Jesus the Christ all bodies can serve as
ways to God, all can be open to and give news of the divine
presence.[43]

McFague includes Teilhard among the "great theologians and
poets of the Christian sacramental tradition." Yet she does
him injustice when she maintains that he, like others in the
Christian tradition, "does not underscore the intrinsic value
of all things earthly" but only appreciates the symbolic importance of each and every body on earth.[44] From such a perspective the things of this earth are not loved for themselves
but are principally appreciated "*as expressions of* divine
beauty, sustenance, truth and glory."[45] When some sentences
of Teilhard's are taken in isolation, one may sometimes get
this impression, but McFague's mistaken assessment is not
borne out within the wider context of his work where he often stresses the *intrinsic* value of all things earthly and of all
our efforts and achievements.

Unlike many other theologians, Teilhard understood the
words of St. John's Gospel "And the Word was made Flesh"
(John 1:14) in a very realistic, concrete and bodily sense, so
much so that for him the whole universe "is seen to be a
flesh."[46] The universal, cosmic Christ is the center of the universe, the center of humanity and the center of each person.
This is why he speaks of the "heart"—the heart of matter, the
heart of the world, the heart of humanity. Teilhard is truly a
physical realist in his understanding of the biblical passages
about the presence of God in the world. In fact, in one of his
retreat notes he refers to the "pan-presence of Christ"[47] and
this presence is symbolized by the heart. It is in Christ's heart
that all the physical and spiritual realities of the world come
together, in one particular person to whom all things are related, so that this divine person is at the same time a cosmic
person and one of the most intimate nearness to the human

being. From Christ's heart radiates love for the whole world and for all its realities. Our growth, our energies, our efforts, all our work, contribute to both the building of the world and the building-up of the body of Christ.

One can say, as Anne Hunt Overzee has done, that "Teilhard revisioned 'the body of Christ' for himself and for his times, using tools drawn from contemporary sources, both Christian and non-Christian. Clearly one such tool was evolutionary theory; another was philosophical science. It could be said that the breadth of Teilhard's vision could not be encompassed by existing theological language. He needed to create his own synthesis of traditional symbolism and contemporary thought to express his own world view centered on a cosmic Christ."[48] For him, seeing Christ in all things was the most powerful source for Christian renewal, for the transformation of humanity and the responsible, reverential care of our planet. His deeply mystical faith was a fervent faith in Christ, a faith steeped in and shaped by eucharistic and sacramental spirituality, nourished by all those elements that are most distinctively Christian.

One of the greatest challenges today is to find what might be called "a spirituality-of-being-in-the-world," a deeply reflective, responsible and responsive spirituality that addresses itself to the practical problems and tasks of our world. Many traditional spiritualities are indeed unconnected to the world as a whole, or to the everyday world of our lives. In many ways traditional spirituality has to be reconceived and revisioned in order to become a true leaven of life.

Teilhard's spiritual vision was centered on and rooted in Christ. Christians can be greatly inspired by the immense power of this faith, the strength of his courage, the beauty of his saintliness and the sincerity of his devotion. Believers of other faiths and none, even though they do not share his devotion to the spirit of Christ, may yet be drawn into the great power of his vision, which trusted and praised the powers of all life, of cosmic life, which he saw as life divine.

In one sense Teilhard's vision was a uniquely personal one, the quintessence of his own longings, searches, sufferings and loves. Yet he also knew that the importance and strength of this vision transcended the limits of his own life, that it could fire people's imagination, inspire their efforts and give them hope. He once said that his mission would only be fulfilled to the extent that others went beyond him. His vision of the dignity of human life embedded in the larger web of cosmic life, his emphasis on global responsibility, action and choice in shaping the future of humanity on our planet, and the need for life-affirming spiritual goals, can inspire people of all beliefs and none. For Christians Teilhard de Chardin is a remarkable, shining example of creative Christian renewal that believes in life, affirms life as a task to be done, a work to be achieved, and celebrates life as a most precious and wonderful gift to be loved and experienced as a sign of the Spirit who sustains us all.

Epilogue

It has not been possible to deal in this book with all the themes in Teilhard de Chardin's large oeuvre that have a bearing on spirituality. This is especially true of the large role the future occupies in his thought, and also his important reflections on the "rise of the masses," the significance of the development of human collectivities at a global level. Both these themes have implications for the full development of a modern "spirituality-of-being-in-the-world," as have our attitudes toward work and time.

Also deeply important is his understanding of and great capacity for friendship and human affection. His close friendship with women was so decisive in his own development that it is impossible to interpret Teilhard's reflections on love and union without reference to the place he assigns to the feminine as a unitive element.[1] Absolutely central is the key correspondence of *The Letters of Teilhard de Chardin and Lucile Swan.*[2] Written between the years 1932 and 1955, these letters provide many key insights into the way Teilhard worked and lived, loved and prayed, was creative and suffered. They are an impressive testimony and proof of "the massive psychological integration,"[3] the consistence and coherence the Christian faith provided for all the ups and downs of Teilhard's own life. The discovery of a deeply spiritual and mystical vision, of "a Christic beyond Christ,"[4] never ceased to fill him with "delight," "passion" and "wonder."[5] He felt it was his life's vocation to pass on "the flame of Christianity"[6] so that others might be nourished and sustained by the same faith, set aflame by the same spirit.

The world-affirming quality of Teilhard's spirituality bears the hallmark of Ignatian spirituality with its emphasis to find

God in *all* things, not only in a religious context, in prayer and meditation, but in all human experiences and activities. Jesuit spirituality has a very active character, and Teilhard represents this spirituality in a decidedly modern form. But many other parallels with Teilhard's spirituality and mysticism can be found in the history of spirituality. Orthodox theology speaks of the vision of divine light whereby the mystic is kindled into flame by the fire of the Godhead; Brother Lawrence teaches the "practice of the presence of God" amid all things; and closer to our own time Simone Weil finds God waiting among suffering and affliction, and describes Christ's presence filling her with infinity and silence beyond the absence of sound. These and other parallels are worth exploring.

Teilhard's methodology was not traditional. His favorite mode of expression was the more provisional and experimental mode of the essay, perhaps an ideal postmodern form, always open-ended, always striving for completion while remaining incomplete. It is a most appropriate form for experimenting with new words, new concepts, a new vision of the world that others can explore, play with and push to further limits, to new horizons. Teilhard's work contains a profusion of ideas and images that provide creative elements for a new metaphorical theology. As Sallie McFague has said, such a theology is always "at risk."[7] But anyone willing to take such risk can discover a divine "Ocean of Life"[8] and develop a new wholeness and holiness while actively committed and fully involved with the world of our time.

Abbreviations

LTF   Pierre Teilhard de Chardin. *Letters to Two Friends 1926-1952*. London: Collins Fontana, 1972.

MD   Pierre Teilhard de Chardin. *Le Milieu Divin: An Essay on the Interior Life*. London: Collins, 1963.

MPN   Pierre Teilhard de Chardin. *Man's Place in Nature*. London: Collins, 1966.

PM   Pierre Teilhard de Chardin. *The Phenomenon of Man*. London: Collins, 1959.

SC   Pierre Teilhard de Chardin. *Science and Christ*. London: Collins, 1968.

TF   Pierre Teilhard de Chardin. *Toward the Future*. London: Collins, 1975.

VP   Pierre Teilhard de Chardin. *The Vision of the Past*. London: Colllins, 1966.

WTW   Pierre Teilhard de Chardin. *Writings in Time of War*. London: Collins, 1968.

Notes

1. Christian Spirituality Today

[1]HM, 209; my translation. The English title "Note on the Presentation of the Gospel in a New Age" does not fully reflect the French original.

[2]HM, 210; my translation.

[3]SC, 220.

[4]SC, 221.

[5]L. Dupré and Don E. Saliers, eds., *Christian Spirituality: Post-Reformation and Modern* (London: SCM, 1990; New York: The Crossroad Publishing Company, 1989), xiii.

[6]This society "exists to promote research and dialogue within the growing interdisciplinary field of spirituality" (*Christian Spirituality Bulletin*, 1/1 [Spring 1993], 2). It originated from a consultation held in 1982, and since 1992 it organizes regular meetings during the annual meeting of the American Academy of Religion.

[7]*The Way Supplement* 1995/84, available from The Way Publications, 114 Mount Street, London, W1Y, 6AN.

[8]Published in the United States by the Crossroad Publishing Company; in Britain some volumes are published by Routledge & Kegan Paul, others by SCM Press.

[9]Quoted from the volume edited by Bernard McGinn and John Meyendorff, *Christian Spirituality: Origins to the Twelfth Century* (London: Routledge & Kegan Paul, 1986; New York: The Crossroad Publishing Company, 1985), xiiif.

[10]See the pupil resource book and teacher handbook *Looking Inwards, Looking Outwards: Exploring Life's Possibilities* (Derby: Christian Education Movement, 1997, sponsored by the John Templeton Foundation). For further information contact CEM, Royal Buildings, Victoria Street, Derby DE1 1GW, England.

[11]OED (1970, vol. 10: 624).

[12]In *Christian Spirituality Bulletin*, 1/2 (Fall 1993), 11.

[13]This is taken from a publication of the British Office for Standards in Education (OFSTED), "Framework for the Inspection of Schools," Section 5.1, August 1993, quoted in *Working Guidelines* of the Templeton Project, 2.11.95. See also the helpful article by Clive Beck, "Education for Spirituality," *Interchange* 17/2 (1986), 148-156, published by the Ontario Institute for Studies in Education, Canada. For more details on children's spirituality, examined in relation to Christian, Islamic, Jewish and secular concerns, see the fine study by Robert Coles, *The Spiritual Lives of Children* (Boston: Houghton Mifflin Company and London: HarperCollins, 1990). There also exists a new journal devoted

to this subject, *The International Journal of Children's Spirituality*, published by the Chichester Institute of Higher Education, England.

[14]Sandra Schneiders, *Christian Spirituality Bulletin* 1/2 (Fall 1993), 11.

[15]An exception is the well-known French *Dictionnaire de Spiritualité* (Paris: Beauchesne, 1991), which devotes a long entry to Teilhard de Chardin (see vol. XV: cols. 115-126).

[16]HM, 210.

[17]CU, 388.

[18]See his motto for the essay "Cosmic Life," WTW, 14.

[19]Quoted in André Dupleix, *Prier 15 Jours avec Pierre Teilhard de Chardin* (Paris: Nouvelle Cité, 1994), 20.

[20]HM, 93.

[21]LT, 86.

[22]LT, 85f.

[23]AE, 405.

[24]TF, 164.

[25]Quoted in HU, 70.

2. "Rediscovering Fire"

[1]HM, 210.

[2]Cf. "Breathe on me, Breath of God,
      Till I am wholly thine,
      Until this earthly part of me
      Glows with the fire divine." (See Hymn No. 342, verse 3 in the *New English Hymnal,* Norwich: The Canterbury Press, 1988, 502.)

[3]TF, 87.

[4]See Ursula King, *Spirit of Fire: The Life and Vision of Teilhard de Chardin* (Maryknoll, NY: Orbis Books, 1996). The present chapter draws on some material in that book but sets it in a wider context. The experiences and events of Teilhard's life are described in much more detail in the biography.

[5]HM, 61.

[6]HM, 74.

[7]HM, 15.

[8]The English translation appeared only in 1978.

[9]HM, 198.

[10]See HU, 27.

[11]See HM, 15 and 16.

[12]HM, 47.

[13]Gaston Bachelard, *The Psychoanalysis of Fire* (Boston: Beacon Press, 1964).

[14]Ibid., 110.

[15]Ibid., 55, 16.

[16]WTW, 14.

[17]Ibid.; partly my translation.

[18]WTW, 61.

[19]WTW, 70.

[20]LT, 202. Addressed to Abbé Breuil in March 1934, these words were written after the death of Teilhard's friend and close collaborator, Davidson Black, whose loss greatly affected Teilhard.

[21]HU, 41. Given the central role the heart of Christ plays in Teilhard's devotion and thought, it is understandable why the German scholar Karl Schmitz Moormann assigns a key role to this mystical experience in Teilhard's inner development; see his study *Pierre Teilhard de Chardin: Evolution—die Schöpfung Gottes* (Mainz: Matthias Grünewald Verlag, 1996), 103f. However, in my view it is a mistake to reduce Teilhard's encounter with mysticism to this one experience of contemplating a painting of Christ. His mystical experiences are diverse, complex and cumulative, as I have tried to show in my earlier book *Towards a New Mysticism: Teilhard de Chardin and Eastern Religions* (London: Collins and New York: Seabury Press, 1980).

[22]HU, 43.

[23]HU, 49.

[24]Ibid.

[25]HU, 50.

[26]WTW, 223.

[27]WTW, 204, 206.

[28]WTW, 217.

[29]HM, 204.

[30]MD, 122.

[31]HM, 207. This is a passage from his early essay "My Universe" (1918). Another very important essay of the same title was written in 1924; see SC, 37-85.

[32]MD, 27.

[33]MD, 137

[34]MD, 14.

[35]MD, 16.

[36]For a recent South African study of Smuts's thought see Piet Beukes, *The Holistic Smuts: A Study in Personality* (Cape Town: Human & Rousseau, second edition, 1991).

[37]FM, 54f.

[38]SC, 75.

[39]HU, 21.

[40]PM, 295f.

[41]MD, 138.

[42]See HE, 19-47.

[43]The quotations are from HE, 32, 33, 34, 35.

[44]Evelyn Underhill, *Mystics of the Church* (London: J. Clarke & Co., 1925), 12.

[45]Eva Hoffman, *Lost in Translation* (London: Minerva, 1989), 154.

3. *Spirituality and Evolution*

[1]Henri de Lubac dedicated his book *The Religion of Teilhard de Chardin* (London: Collins, 1967) "To the memory of a great contemplative Père Charles Nicolet (1896-1961) who was a devoted friend of Père

Teilhard , and *was consumed by the same fire*" (emphasis added).

[2]See Chap. 12, "Pierre Teilhard de Chardin's *Le Milieu Divin*" in Donald M. MacKinnon, *Themes in Theology: The Three-Fold Cord* (Edinburgh: T. & T. Clark, 1987), 189-195.

[3]Charles Raven, *Teilhard de Chardin: Scientist and Seer* (London: Collins, 1962).

[4]MacKinnon, op. cit., 193.

[5]MacKinnon, op. cit., 194.

[6]Dorothy Emmet, "Editorial" in *Theoria to Theory*, 14/4 (1981), 269.

[7]MacKinnon, op. cit., 192.

[8]See David Tracy, "Recent Catholic Spirituality: Unity amid Diversity," in Louis Dupré and Don E. Saliers, eds., *Christian Spirituality: Post-Reformation and Modern* (London: SCM, 1990; New York: The Crossroad Publishing Company, 1989), 143-173. The quotations are taken from page 155.

[9]Ibid., 153f.

[10]Thomas Corbishley, *The Spirituality of Teilhard de Chardin* (London: Collins, Fontana, 1971), 7.

[11]Ibid., back cover.

[12]See R. C. Zaehner's comparative study *Evolution in Religion: A Study in Sri Aurobindo and Pierre Teilhard de Chardin* (Oxford: Clarendon Press, 1971).

[13]Teilhard explained his philosophy of creative union in his essay "My Universe" written in 1924; see SC, 37-85. For a detailed study of what Teilhard meant by "creative union" see Donald Gray, *The One and the Many: Teilhard de Chardin's Vision of Unity* (London: Collins, 1969).

[14]SC, 15.

[15]Personal communication. Endorsement written for the publication of my Teilhard biography *The Spirit of Fire*.

[16]MD, 31.

[17]For a detailed discussion of Teilhard's thought on personalization and socialization, on individual and community, see chap. 2 "Socialization and the Future of Humankind" and chap. 3 "The One and the Many" in my *The Spirit of One Earth: Reflections on Teilhard de Chardin and Global Spirituality* (New York: Paragon House, 1989), 29-43, 45-63.

[18]See MPN, 13 and 17.

[19]PM, 42.

[20]See HE, 93-112; the original French title means simply "The Spiritual Phenomenon."

[21]See PM, 62-66.

[22]PM, 62, 63.

[23]AE, 236, 238.

[24]See AE, 238, 239.

[25]This is the literal translation of the French "Le Phénomène Spirituel." For the English translation "The Phenomenon of Spirituality," see HE, 93-112 and my discussion of this essay in U. King, *The Spirit of One Earth*, 65-82.

[26]See his essay "The Sense of Man" (1929) in TF, 13-39.

[27]HE, 19-47.
[28]HE, 19.
[29]HE, 37f.
[30]HE, 93.
[31]HE, 104, 105.
[32]HE, 106.
[33]See HE, 106f.
[34]HE, 110.
[35]HE, 112.

[36]For further texts on energy see Teilhard's essays "Human Energy" (1937), HE, 113-162; "The Spiritual Energy of Suffering" (1951), AE, 245-249; "The Reflection of Energy" (1952), AE, 319-337; "The Energy of Evolution" (1953), AE, 359-372; "The Activation of Human Energy" (1953), AE, 385-393.

[37]See MD, 36-43.
[38]MD, 42.
[39]MD, 43.
[40]HE, 48-52.
[41]HE, 48, 51.

[42]Dame Cicely Saunders, the founder of the Hospice Movement, mentioned in a radio interview some years ago how much she had been inspired in her work for the terminally ill by Teilhard's views on suffering.

[43]HE, 153.
[44]Ibid.
[45]HE, 135.
[46]HE, 136.
[47]HE, 153.
[48]FM, 147.
[49]Ibid., 146.
[50]CE, 152.

[51]All quotations are taken from the essay "Human Energy" in HE, 153.

[52]See FM, 140-148.
[53]FM, 148.
[54] *Times Higher Education Supplement* 24/6 (1994).
[55]AE, 242.
[56]PM, 296.
[57]CE, 161.
[58]SC, 38.
[59]Ibid., 38, 39.
[60]MD, 126, 128.

4. Christ in All Things

[1]See A. McGrath, *The Christian Theology Reader* (Oxford: Blackwell, 1995). There is also no reference to Teilhard's ideas in Gareth Jones, *Critical Theology* (Cambridge: Polity Press, 1995), although this work

deals at length with dynamic christology and also with spirituality.

[2]J. A. Lyons, *The Cosmic Christ in Origen and Teilhard de Chardin: A Comparative Study* (Oxford: Oxford University Press, 1982), 4. For an excellent study of Teilhard's christology see Christopher F. Mooney, *Teilhard de Chardin and the Mystery of Christ* (London: Collins, 1966).

[3]CE, 98f. This passage, taken from Teilhard's important essay "How I Believe" (1934), is also quoted by Mooney, ibid., 49, whose translation I have followed in part.

[4]WTW, 15.

[5]WTW, 25, 26, 27; cf. MD, 54f.

[6]WTW, 27.

[7]WTW, 16.

[8]WTW, 15.

[9]See HM, 16, 47.

[10]CE, 244. The rich symbolism of the divine heart as heart of the world and Teilhard's great devotion to the Sacred Heart of Jesus cannot be discussed here, but see the article by Robert Faricy, S.J., "The Heart of Christ in the Spirituality of Teilhard de Chardin," *Gregorianum* 69/2 (1988), 261-77.

[11]CE, 243.

[12]See CE, 237-243.

[13]CE, 237.

[14]SC, 112.

[15]CE, 241, 242.

[16]There exists considerable literature on this topic. For one of the most recent discussions see John Hick, *The Metaphor of God Incarnate: Christology in a Pluralistic Age* (Louisville, Kentucky: Westminster/ John Knox Press, 1993). There is no mention of Teilhard in this work.

[17]In HU, 23.

[18]HU, 27.

[19]WTW, 147.

[20]WTW, 146, 147.

[21]WTW, 146.

[22]CE, 182f.

[23]CE, 183n.

[24]All quotations are from *The Mass on the World;* see HU, 32.

[25]HU, 33.

[26]See Anne Hunt Overzee, *The Body Divine: The Symbol of the Body in the Works of Teilhard de Chardin and Ramanuja* (Cambridge: Cambridge University Press, 1992).

[27]HU, 33.

[28]HU, 35.

[29]Ibid.

[30]HU, 34.

[31]See SC, 59; 124; also CE, 129 and HM, 55.

[32]For a critical edition of the text and its interpretation see George E. Ganss, S.J., ed., *Ignatius of Loyola: The Spiritual Exercises and Selected Works* (New York: Paulist Press, 1991), 9; published in the series

The Classics of Western Spirituality.

[33]London: Collins, 1966.

[34]See ibid., chap.VI, 189ff.

[35]See note 2.

[36]Lyons, op. cit., 219.

[37]HU, 121; the quotation is from the essay "Cosmic Life."

[38]LTF, 48.

[39]WTW, 177-190.

[40]WTW, 189.

[41]See his "Note on the Universal Christ" (1920) in SC, 14-20.

[42]SC, 14.

[43]SC, 19.

[44]SC, 54.

[45]SC, 57; see his entire essay "My Universe" from which this quotation is taken.

[46]SC, 164.

[47]SC, 167.

[48]SC, 166, 167.

[49]TF, 35.

[50]CE, 126.

[51]CE, 127f.

[52]CE, 129.

[53]SC, 124.

[54]See his remark of 1926 quoted in LLZ, 34.

[55]Quoted in LLZ, 34f.

[56]Quoted in LLZ, 35.

[57]SC, 124.

[58]See for example his reference to "new theological orientations," CE, 173, 176.

[59]See CE, 183, the section "A New Mystical Orientation," written in 1945.

[60]SC, 126.

[61]CE, 94.

[62]Ewert H.Cousins, *Christ of the 21st Century* (Rockport, MA: Element Books, 1992); see especially his section "Teilhard's Christology," 176-178.

[63]CE, 167.

[64]HM, 98.

[65]HM, 55, 57f.

5. *Mysticism-in-Action*

[1]VP, 181.

[2]VP, 182.

[3]CE, 176.

[4]CE, 242.

[5]CE, 243.

[6]MD, 118.

[7]See CE, 59, 58.

[8]CE, 58f. This quotation comes from an important essay, "Pantheism and Christianity," written in 1923.

[9]Maréchal's diverse articles on different mystics were later collected together under the title *Études sur la Psychologie des Mystiques* (Paris: Desclée, 1924) and translated as *Studies in the Psychology of the Mystics* (London: Burns & Oates, 1927; enlarged second edition, 2 vols., Louvain, 1937-38). Teilhard read and made extensive notes on the English translation during 1945.

[10]These are discussed in the Appendix of my *Towards a New Mysticism: Teilhard de Chardin and Eastern Religions* (London: Collins and New York: Seabury Press, 1980), 238-47.

[11]R. C. Zaehner, *Evolution in Religion* (Oxford: Clarendon Press, 1971), 6.

[12]WTW, 28.

[13]*Journal,* 27; my translation.

[14]WTW, 14.

[15]SC, 77.

[16]SC, 75f.

[17]A critical discussion of these terms is found in my *Towards a New Mysticism* (see n. 10), especially in chap. 6. See also my article "Teilhard's Reflections on Eastern Religions Revisited," *Zygon: Journal of Religion and Science* 30/1 (1995), 45-70.

[18]See R. C. Zaehner, *Mysticism, Sacred and Profane: An Inquiry into Some Varieties of Praeternatural Experience* (Oxford: Clarendon Press, 1957).

[19]See R. C. Zaehner, "Teilhard and Eastern Religions," *The Teilhard Review* 2 (1967-68), 43.

[20]AE, 56.

[21]See "Some Notes on the Mystical Sense: An Attempt at Clarification" in TF, 209-211.

[22]Perhaps he is expressing a doubt here about his own oversimplification.

[23]TF, 209.

[24]TF, 210.

[25]My translation of the French title "Recherche, Travail et Adoration." The English version was published as "Research, Work and Worship" in SC, 214-20.

[26]Published in HM, 80-102.

[27]Quoted in HM, 80.

[28]MD, 118.

[29]HM, 100.

[30]HM, 83. All quotations in this paragraph are taken from the essay "The Christic."

[31]HM, 83.

[32]HM, 101.

[33]HM, 100. Note here the implicit reference to the burning bush, which figured as the title to the Introduction of his earlier spiritual

essay, "The Heart of Matter" (1950). In "The Christic" (1955) it is the coming down from the mountain, the return to the world after having seen God.

[34]These arguments are presented at the end of "The Christic"; see HM, 100-102.

[35]HM, 96.

[36]HM, 99.

[37]HM, 102.

[38]"I can tell you that I now live permanently in the presence of God," Teilhard is reported to have said in December 1954 to his friend Leroy; see LF, 225.

[39]F. C. Happold, *Mysticism: A Study and an Anthology* (Harmondsworth: Pelican Books, 1971), 394, 395.

[40]HE, 163-181.

[41]SC, 199-205.

[42]HE, 163f.

[43]HE, 180, 181.

[44]SC, 201.

[45]SC, 201f.

[46]Excerpts from an unpublished, cyclostyled report of a discussion held at a meeting of the Union des Croyants, the French branch of the World Congress of Faiths, in Paris in 1948; see pages 30, 37, 38; my translation.

[47]LF, 193; my translation.

[48]SC, 112.

[49]See LI, 450, 460.

[50]AE, 227.

[51]SC, 75.

6. Interfaith Dialogue and Christian Spirituality

[1]For a detailed account of the sixty years' history of this organization see Marcus Braybrooke, *A Wider Vision; A History of the World Congress of Faiths* (Oxford: Oneworld, 1996).

[2]For a contemporary account and critical appraisal of the 1893 World's Parliament of Religions see Richard Hughes Seager, ed., *The Dawn of Religious Pluralism: Voices from the World's Parliament of Religions, 1893* (La Salle/Ill.: Open Court, 1993) and Eric J. Ziolkowski, ed., *A Museum of Faiths: Histories and Legacies of the 1893 World's Parliament of Religions* (Atlanta/GA: Scholars Press, 1993). A comprehensive history of the interfaith movement is found in Marcus Braybrooke, *Pilgrimage of Hope: One Hundred Years of Global Interfaith Dialogue* (London: SCM Press, 1992).

[3]For example, one of the roots of the World Congress of Faiths was the "Religions of the Empire" conference held in London in 1924 whereas the World's Parliament of Religions, held in Chicago in 1893, was occasioned by the World's Columbian Exposition, organized to celebrate the four-hundredth anniversary of Christopher Columbus's "discovery" of

the New World.

[4]See "Teilhard's Reflections on Eastern Religions Revisited," *Zygon: Journal of Religion and Science* 30/1 (1995), 45-70, and especially *Towards a New Mysticism: Teilhard de Chardin and Eastern Religions* (London: Collins and New York: Seabury Press, 1980).

[5]SC, 99, 100.

[6]SC, 102.

[7]TF, 141.

[8]See Hans Küng and Karl-Josef Kuschel, eds., *A Global Ethic: The Declaration of the Parliament of the World's Religions* (London: SCM Press, 1993).

[9]See CE, 121, n.8.

[10]See SC, 104f.

[11]Braybrooke, in his history of the World Congress of Faiths, *A Wider Vision* (see n. 1), does not mention these details but states only that the *Union des Croyants* "had the support of Teilhard de Chardin" (66) and that Teilhard "was sympathetic to the aims of the WCF" (161).

[12]For a detailed discussion of Teilhard's contributions to the *Union des Croyants* see chap. 8, "Teilhard's Association with the World Congress of Faiths, 1947-1950" in U. King, *The Spirit of One Earth* (New York: Paragon House, 1989), 135-46.

[13]FM, 196-200.

[14]From an unpublished discussion available only in cyclostyled form.

[15]AE, 239f.

[16]HM, 91.

[17]AE, 241.

[18]AE, 242.

[19]Ibid.

[20]See Samuel Rayan, "The Search for an Asian Spirituality of Liberation," in Virginia Fabella, Peter K. H. Lee, and David Kwang-sun Suh, eds., *Asian Christian Spirituality: Reclaiming Traditions* (Maryknoll, NY: Orbis Books, 1992), 20.

[21]Rayan, op. cit., 22.

[22]See Fabella et al., op. cit., 3.

7. *Third World Theology and the Voices of Women*

[1]MD, 138.

[2]John Robinson, *Exploration into God* (Stanford: Stanford University Press, 1967).

[3]Robinson, op. cit., 132.

[4]MD, 138f.

[5]MD, 139.

[6]Ibid.

[7]MD, 139f.

[8]AE, 59-75.

[9]AE, 74.

[10]AE, 74f.

[11]MD, 138.

[12]See Virginia Fabella and Sergio Torres, eds., *Irruption of the Third World: Challenge to Theology* (Maryknoll, NY: Orbis Books, 1983).

[13]Ibid., xii.

[14]Ibid., 195, 197, 204.

[15]Ibid., 204.

[16]Ibid., 136.

[17]See Tosh Arai and Wesley Ariarajah, eds., *Spirituality in Interfaith Dialogue* (Geneva: WCC Publications, and Maryknoll, NY: Orbis Books, 1989).

[18]Ibid., vi.

[19]See the published proceedings edited by K. C. Abraham and Bernadette Mbuy-Beya, *Spirituality of the Third World: A Cry for Life* (Maryknoll, NY: Orbis Books, 1994).

[20]Ibid., 197, 198.

[21]Ibid., 199f.

[22]Ibid., 200.

[23]For Asian examples of such "reclaiming" see Fabella, et al., op. cit.

[24]Abraham & Mbuy-Beya, op. cit., 188, 189.

[25]See the final statement of the 1992 Nairobi conference with its section "The Irruption of Women: A Cry for Life" in Abraham and Mbuy-Beya, op. cit., 192f.

[26]See Kari E. Børresen, ed., *The Image of God: Gender Models in Judaeo-Christian Tradition* (Minneapolis: Fortress Press, 1995) and her article "Women's Studies of the Christian Tradition: New Perspectives" in Ursula King, ed., *Religion and Gender* (Oxford: Blackwell, 1995), 245-55.

[27]See the survey on the different geographical, religious and theoretical sites of the feminist struggle provided by Elisabeth Schüssler Fiorenza and M. Shawn Copeland, eds., "Feminist Theology in Different Contexts," *Concilium* 1996/1 (London: SCM Press and Maryknoll, NY: Orbis Books).

[28]See her "Reflections from a Third World Woman's Perspective: Women's Experience and Liberation Theologies" in Virginia Fabella and Sergio Torres, eds., *Irruption of the Third World: Challenge to Theology* (Maryknoll, NY: Orbis Books, l983), 246-55.

[29]For an overview see my Introduction in the reader I edited, *Feminist Theology from the Third World* (London: SPCK and Maryknoll, NY: Orbis Books, 1994); a full historical account of women's work in EATWOT is given by one of the central participants, Virginia Fabella, in her *Beyond Bonding: A Third World Women's Theological Journey* (Manila: Ecumenical Association of Third World Theologians and the Institute of Women's Studies, 1993). A dialogue between Third World and First World women theologians took place in Costa Rica in 1994; see Mary John Mananzan et al., eds., *Women Resisting Violence: Spirituality for Life* (Maryknoll, NY: Orbis Books, 1996).

[30]See Elsa Tamez, ed., *Through Her Eyes: Women's Theology from Latin America* (Maryknoll, NY: Orbis Books, 1989).

[31]This is the title of the documentary film made by the WCC about the work of the Korean woman theologian Chung Hyun Kyung.

[32]Virginia Fabella and Mercy Amba Oduyoye, eds., *With Passion and Compassion: Third World Women Doing Theology* (Maryknoll, NY: Orbis Books, 1988).

[33]María Clara Bingemer, "Women in the Future of the Theology of Liberation," in Marc H. Ellis and Otto Maduro, eds., *The Future of Liberation Theology: Essays in Honor of Gustavo Gutiérrez* (Maryknoll, NY: Orbis Books, 1990), 478.

[34]Ibid., 479.

[35]Ibid., 480.

[36]See Chung Hyun Kyung, *Struggle to Be the Sun Again: Introducing Asian Women's Theology* (Maryknoll, NY: Orbis Books, 1990; London: SCM Press, 1991), especially chap. 7 where she discusses a new understanding of theology and of the identity of theologians.

[37]Bingemer, op. cit., 481.

[38]I have demonstrated this at length in my *Women and Spirituality: Voices of Protest and Promise* (London: Macmillan and University Park, PA: Penn State Press, second edition, 1993).

[39]See María Pilar Aquino, *Our Cry for Life: Feminist Theology from Latin America* (Maryknoll, NY: Orbis Books, 1993).

[40]See Chung, op. cit., see note 36.

[41]Chung, op. cit., 114.

[42]See the full text of her address "Come Holy Spirit—Renew the Whole Creation" in the official Assembly Report edited by Michael Kinnamon, *Signs of the Spirit* (Geneva: WCC Publications, 1991), 37-47. A shorter version can be found in Ursula King, ed., *Feminist Theology from the Third World*; 392-94.

[43]Notes from a lecture given at the University of Bristol, "Women Shape Their World," May 15, 1994.

[44]See his texts in HU.

8. Christian Spirituality

[1]LAG, 80.

[2]See Mary Tardiff, ed., *At Home in the World: The Letters of Thomas Merton & Rosemary Radford Ruether* (Maryknoll, NY: Orbis Books, 1995), 8f.

[3]Ibid., 6.

[4]Julian Huxley, *Memories II* (London: George Allen & Unwin, 1973), 29, 28.

[5]Ibid., 29.

[6]Ibid., 30.

[7]Ibid., 28.

[8]This is not the place to provide detailed statistics on ecological crises or the evils of war, but it is worth pointing out that in early 1996 there were about 11 wars raging in Africa alone (as reported in the German newspaper *Frankfurter Allgemeine* on April 13, 1996). The

pacifist Fellowship of Reconciliation, founded during the First World War, calculated before the wars in former Yugoslavia had begun that 227 wars have been fought during the twentieth century, and estimated that a total of 107.8 million human beings were killed during this century.

[9]Hans Küng and Karl-Josef Kuschel, eds., *A Global Ethic: The Declaration of the Parliament of the World's Religions* (London: SCM Press, 1993), 26.

[10]Independent Commission on Population and Quality of Life, *Caring for the Future: Making the Next Decades Provide a Life Worth Living* (Oxford and New York: Oxford University Press, 1996).

[11]Ibid., 296.

[12]See Samuel Rayan, "Theological Perspectives on the Environmental Crisis" in R. S. Sugiratharajah, ed., *Frontiers in Asian Christian Theology: Emerging Trends* (Maryknoll, NY: Orbis Books, 1994), 221-236.

[13]Ibid., 224.

[14]Ibid., 225.

[15]Ibid., 226.

[16]For a wide-ranging survey of these developments see the volume edited by David G. Hallman, *Ecotheology: Voices from South and North* (Geneva: WCC Publications and Maryknoll, NY: Orbis Books, 1994).

[17]Hallman's book contains a section on ecofeminism, but for women's voices from the South see especially Rosemary Radford Ruether, ed., *Women Healing Earth: Third World Women on Ecology, Feminism, and Religion* (Maryknoll, NY: Orbis Books, 1996; London: SCM Press, 1996).

[18]See Thomas Berry, "Ecology and the Future of Catholicism: A Statement of the Problem" in Albert J. Lachance and John Carroll, eds., *Embracing Earth: Catholic Approaches to Ecology* (Maryknoll, NY: Orbis Books, 1994), xii.

[19]Henryk Skolimoski, "Ecological Spirituality and Its Practical Consequences," *The Teilhard Review* 27/2 (1992), 43-53.

[20]Ibid., 47.

[21]Ibid., 46.

[22]Carol Adams, ed., *Ecofeminism and the Sacred* (New York: Continuum, 1993).

[23]Eleanor Rae, *Women, the Earth, the Divine* (Maryknoll, NY: Orbis Books, 1994).

[24]See also Rosemary Ruether, *Gaia and God: An Ecofeminist Theology of Earth Healing* (HarperSanFrancisco, 1992; London: SCM Press, 1993).

[25]Allerd Stikker, *The Transformation Factor: Towards an Ecological Consciousness* (Rockport, Massachusetts and Shaftesbury, Devon: Element Books, 1992). See also Charlene Spretnak, *The Spiritual Dimension of Green Politics* (Santa Fe, NM: Bear & Company, 1986).

[26]Quoted by William J. Wood, S.J. in Albert J. Lachance & John E. Carroll, eds., *Embracing the Earth: Catholic Approaches to Ecology* (Maryknoll, NY: Orbis Books, 1994), 189.

[27]See especially his essay written in 1931, "The Spirit of the Earth," HE, 19-47.

[28]Bernice Marie-Daly, "Ecofeminism: Sacred Matter/Sacred Mother," *Teilhard Studies* 25 (Chambersburg, PA: Anima Books and the American Teilhard Association for the Future of Man, Autumn 1991), 1.

[29]Marti Kheel, quoted in ibid., 2.

[30]Quoted in HU, 75.

[31]Quoted in HU, 88, from a passage in *The Future of Man*.

[32]MPN, 117.

[33]MPN, 118.

[34]Ibid.

[35]MPN, 119, 120.

[36]MPN, 121.

[37]Ruether, op. cit.; see note 24.

[38]Ibid., 243.

[39]Ibid., 245.

[40]As quoted in HU, 130f. and 131f.

[41]Sally McFague, *The Body of God: An Ecological Theology* (Minneapolis: Fortress Press, 1993; London: SCM Press, 1993).

[42]Ibid., 14.

[43]Ibid., 184.

[44]Ibid., 185.

[45]Ibid., 184.

[46]SC, 77. The quotation is taken from his important essay "My Universe" (1924).

[47]The expression is found in his retreat notes of 1948 and is discussed by R. Faricy, S.J., in his article "The Heart of Christ in the Spirituality of Teilhard de Chardin," *Gregorianum* 69/2 (1988), 270.

[48]Anne Hunt Overzee, *The Body Divine: The Symbol of the Body in the Works of Teilhard de Chardin and Ramanuja* (Cambridge: Cambridge University Press, 1992), 28f.

Epilogue

[1]I have discussed this in my biography of Teilhard, *Spirit of Fire* (Maryknoll, NY: Orbis Books, 1996); see especially the chapter "Faces of the Feminine."

[2]See Thomas M. King, S.J. and Mary Wood Gilbert, eds., *The Letters of Teilhard de Chardin and Lucile Swan* (Washington, D.C.: Georgetown University Press, 1993). See also U. King, "The Letters of Teilhard de Chardin and Lucile Swan: A Personal Interpretation," *Teilhard Studies 32* (The American Teilhard Assocation for the Future of Man, 1995).

[3]See HM, 80.

[4]See HM, 43.

[5]See HM, 83.

[6]See HM, 90.

[7]Sallie McFague, *Models of God: Theology for an Ecological, Nuclear Age* (London: SCM Press, 1987), 34.

[8]WTW, 146.

Index